Do-it-yourself

RESIDENTIAL LETTINGS

by Tessa Shepperson, BA, LLB

LAW PACK™
GUIDE

About the author

Tessa Shepperson is a solicitor in private practice. She qualified in 1990, and set up her own legal practice, TJ Shepperson, in 1994. Tessa specialises in residential landlord and tenant work and is now concentrating on legal work for private residential landlords. She offers legal services for landlords from her specialist site, Landlord-Law Online (www.landlord-law.co.uk). Tessa lives in Norwich with her husband and son.

Residential Lettings Guide

First edition 2000

Law Pack Publishing Limited
10-16 Cole Street
London SE1 4YH

www.lawpack.co.uk

Printed in Great Britain

ISBN: 1 902646 51 7

Important facts

This **Law Pack** Guide contains the information and instructions for landlords letting residential properties. This Guide is for use in England or Wales. It is not suitable for use in Scotland or Northern Ireland.

The information it contains has been carefully compiled from professional sources, but its accuracy is not guaranteed, as laws and regulations may change or be subject to differing interpretations.

Neither this nor any other publication can take the place of a solicitor on important legal matters. As with any legal matter, common sense should determine whether you need the assistance of a solicitor rather than rely solely on the information and forms in this **Law Pack** Guide.

We strongly urge you to consult a solicitor if:

- substantial amounts of money are involved;
- you do not understand the instructions or are uncertain how to complete and use a form correctly;
- what you want to do is not precisely covered by this Guide;
- trusts or business interests are involved.

Contents

Foreword

As stated in the Introduction to this book, being a residential landlord is not easy, and this has spawned the publication of books and guides that vary in quality, all of which are intended to help landlords. With this in mind, we were apprehensive when asked to review yet another 'practical guide for new and experienced landlords'.

The National Federation of Residential Landlords (NRFL) represents at a national level the interests of small, private landlords throughout the country. It is important that they are well-informed as, together, these landlords form the major part of the private rented sector. The NRFL has in its membership virtually all landlords' associations in the country, and it is through this network of 50 landlords' associations, some with many branches, that landlords are represented at local level.

The NRFL relies on these associations to convey information on letting to individual landlords and any publication that assists local associations to carry out this task is welcome. However, many of these publications are confusing, only providing part of the picture or even are sometimes inaccurate.

It was therefore refreshing to discover this clear and balanced publication. Good information raises standards. In doing so, it not only helps tenants but also makes managing residential lettings easier and more profitable. Residential Lettings really is a useful companion for landlords new to letting, whilst experienced landlords who need to check their knowledge will profit from the information it contains.

The NRFL has no hesitation in recommending this publication to landlords; *Residential Lettings* amounts to a management tool that no landlord should be without.

National Federation of Residential Landlords

Introduction

Being a landlord is not as easy as it may appear. It involves a lot of work yet the general perception of landlords is that they have an easy life getting 'money for nothing'. It is important that landlords realise the extent of the obligations that they are taking on and are aware of their legal responsibilities. Landlords are subject to a plethora of regulations that are regularly amended or added to. Usually they involve penalties for non-compliance. These regulations are intended to protect the tenant; however, they can also protect the landlord to a certain extent because if he complies with them he will have a good defence to any claims that may be made against him by the tenant. Also good-quality properties are more likely to attract good-quality tenants – the 'holy grail' of landlords. The landlord with a good tenant has far, far fewer problems than the landlord with a bad tenant.

This book is intended mainly to be a practical guide for new landlords of short-term residential tenancies, although it will, I hope, be useful to experienced landlords and may also be of interest to tenants. After some initial legal explanation (chapter 2), it aims first to guide you through the things that you should be considering before letting a property, and to help you through the process of getting the property ready for letting, finding a tenant, and making the agreement with the tenant. It then goes on to discuss what happens during a tenancy and what you can do if you have problem tenants. Finally there is some discussion about what happens, or should happen, at the end of a tenancy.

This book is intended to be a general guide only. If you have any special or unusual problem you should not rely solely on this book, but should seek independent legal advice.

For convenience (and for no other reason) 'him', 'he' or 'his' has been used throughout and should be read to include 'her', 'she' or 'hers'.

Acknowledgements

It has been great fun writing this book, and my first thanks should go to my editor, Jamie Ross, for giving me the opportunity to write it.

Part of my research has been talking to landlords and to professionals in relevant fields. I am very grateful to all of them for giving up their time, and this book would not have been possible without them. Any remaining mistakes, however, are mine.

I am particularly indebted to Mike Stimpson and John Stather of the National Federation of Residential Landlords and to Nigel Stringer, all of whom kindly read the manuscript. My grateful thanks also go to all of the following (in no particular order): Colin Lawrence FCIH – Area Manager for Cambridgeshire, Suffolk & Norfolk Rent Service; Bruce Edgington, Solicitor – President, and David Brown FRICS MCIArb – Vice President, Chilterns, Thames & Eastern Rent Assessment Panel; David Bush FRICS – Bush Property Management Ltd; Malcolm Turton – Eastern Landlords Association and National Federation of Residential Landlords; Mike Edmunds – Housing Advisor, Norwich Advice Services; John Spencer – Principal Housing Improvement Officer, Norwich City Council; Paul E Carter – HM Principal Inspector of Health & Safety, Health & Safety Executive, Norwich; Beverley Whittaker – Benefits Manager, Revenue Service, Norwich City Council; David Beard and Jonathan Peddle – Norfolk Trading Standards; Robert Graver – Director, Alan Boswell Insurance Brokers Ltd; Nick Saffell FRICS – Partner, Brown & Co; Sally Baits – Solicitor, Norwich City Council; Ian MacLeod M.I.Fire.E – Fire Safety Officer, Norfolk Fire Service.

I am also indebted to all the various landlords I have known and acted for over the years, and to the landlords in the Eastern Landlords Association who have chatted to me at meetings about their problems and experiences as landlords. Many thanks also to my husband Graeme and my mother for their help and encouragement while I was writing this book.

Tessa Shepperson
July 2000

The legal framework

It is important the landlords understand the basic legal framework and the various types of lettings that exist. This is because these differences have important ramifications and implications for the rights of landlords and tenants. I will be discussing these in more detail at various stages later in the book.

Housing and the rights of tenants have always been important political issues and there have been a series of Acts of Parliament on housing matters over the years. This makes the whole subject legally rather a complex one. A landlord's or tenant's rights will to a large extent depend on the Act of Parliament which regulates the tenancy, which in turn depends upon the date when the tenancy originally started. As this book is aimed at new landlords, I will primarily consider the legal situation for a new tenancy (as opposed to a new agreement for an existing tenancy) created after January 2000. However, most of the general points discussed will still be very relevant for older tenancies and landlords with existing tenants. I will try to indicate in the text where any differences occur to assist landlords of older tenancies.

Licences and tenancies

In landlord and tenant law generally, there is a fundamental difference between a *licence* and a *tenancy*. A licence is where the owner of the property gives someone permission to occupy it. A tenancy is where the tenant acquires a 'legal interest' in the property. This 'legal interest' i.e. the tenancy/lease, is more than just permission to live in the property for a while, it is something that is capable of being bought and sold, and can pass to another person after the initial tenant dies.

Property law being what it is, things are not as simple as that. The various Acts of Parliament which regulate short-term lettings have incorporated a number of rights and obligations into tenancies (and to a much lesser extent, licences) which the landlord is unable to exclude from the letting however much he may want to (and even if the licensee/tenant agrees to their being excluded).

One of the most important rights that a tenant has is 'security of tenure'. This means that he can only be evicted from the property if the landlord follows the procedure laid down in the Act of Parliament which regulates that tenancy. In the 1980s when the Rent Act 1977 applied to most tenancies, it was very difficult (and sometimes impossible) for landlords to evict tenants. Because of this, a landlord would sometimes try to claim that a letting was a licence so he could repossess his property through the courts. But in an important case in 1985, the courts ruled that whether an agreement is a tenancy or a licence depends upon the facts of the case and not what the agreement is called. For example, if the occupier has 'exclusive occupation' of all or part of the property and pays rent, then his occupation is normally deemed to be a tenancy, even if the document is called a 'licence agreement'. However, if the occupier receives services (such as board and cleaning) as in bed-and-breakfast accommodation, then the occupation will usually be a licence.

There is little incentive nowadays for landlords to try to get round the legislation, as they have much greater rights under the Housing Acts 1988 and 1996 which apply to most new tenancies today. In particular, landlords can generally recover possession of their property through the courts. The legislation also implies various 'covenants' (i.e. legal obligations) into tenancies, the most important of which are the landlords' repairing covenants. These are considered further in the book, in particular in chapter 3.

Tenancies will run on until they are specifically ended in a recognised way. The most common ways for a tenancy to end are by what lawyers called 'surrender', i.e. if the tenant vacates/gives up possession of the property, or by the court making an order for possession. This is discussed in more detail in chapters 7 and 8.

The table below sets out some of the most important types of tenancy and licence agreements that exist.

TENANCIES

Assured Tenancy ('AT')
Almost all tenancies that are granted nowadays are assured tenancies. The tenant has exclusive occupation of all or part of the property and the landlord has the right to charge a market rent. The landlord's rights (or 'grounds') to repossess the property are as laid down in the Housing Act 1988, the most important being to recover possession as of right if the tenant falls into rent arrears of more than two months.

Assured Shorthold Tenancy ('AST')
Assured shorthold tenancies are a type or sub-group of assured tenancy, where the landlord has the additional right to recover property at the end of the fixed term, the 'shorthold' ground, provided the proper notices have been served on the tenant. ASTs are the most common type of tenancy granted today, as most tenancies are now automatically ASTs unless the landlord specifies otherwise. **In this book, unless otherwise stated, it is assumed that the tenancy under discussion is an AST.**

Rent Act Tenancies
If a tenancy was granted before 15th January 1989, it will be regulated by the Rent Act 1977. This Act was more favourable to tenants: for example it is more difficult for the landlord to evict tenants, and he can only charge a 'fair rent'. Tenancies under the Rent Act can be either protected or statutory, but for the purposes of this book I will refer to them all as Rent Act tenancies. As Rent Act tenancies are by their nature a shrinking category, less consideration will be given to them in this book. Note that you cannot convert a Rent Act tenancy to an AST by giving the tenant a new fixed-term agreement. Whatever the agreement document states, the tenancy will remain a Rent Act tenancy.

Agricultural tenancies
Agricultural tenancies are not covered in this book.

Company lets
If a property is let to a company as opposed to an individual, then much of the current legislation which protects tenants' rights (e.g. in the Housing Acts 1988 and 1996) will not apply. In the past this was sometimes used as a device to prevent the tenant getting security of tenure. However this is now no longer necessary. It is generally

assumed in this book that the tenant will be an individual and not a company.

LICENCES

Lodgers
This is where someone lets a furnished room in their own home. The lodger has fewer rights (see below) and the landlord can evict him without getting a court order. Income up to a specified limit (currently £4,250) is normally exempt from tax.

Holiday lets
If a property is let for a bona fide holiday, normally for a period of weeks rather than months, then this is deemed to be a licence and the landlord can usually evict the occupiers if they refuse to leave, without getting a court order.

LETTINGS WHICH CAN BE EITHER A TENANCY OR A LICENCE

Houses in Multiple Occupation ('HMOs')
This is where a number of people occupy the same property but do not form a single 'household'. These can be tenancies, e.g. where individuals rent their own room (and have separate tenancy agreements) but share other living accommodation (such as kitchen and bathroom) with other tenants; or licences, e.g. where homeless people are housed in bed-and-breakfast accommodation in a hostel. Local authorities have additional regulatory powers in respect of HMOs to ensure that they are of a proper standard of repair and that facilities are provided to a specified standard.

Employees
If an employee is required to occupy accommodation for the purposes of his employment, then this will be a licence and not a tenancy. Otherwise the accommodation will normally be a tenancy, provided of course that the other elements of a tenancy, as discussed above, apply.

Other
There are always exceptions to the rules. If there is something unusual about your property or the terms upon which you intend to let it, or if the property has a very high value or there is an unusually low rent, you should seek independent legal advice.

Note

This book does not cover tenancies where part of the premises are used for a business, e.g. a manager's flat in licensed premises.

In this book I have primarily concentrated on ASTs. However, I have included comments on ATs, Rent Act tenancies, and licences where appropriate.

Resident landlords

Where the owner of the property lives in the same building, a letting is generally excluded from the definition of an AT (or AST). However, the resident landlord rules cannot apply if the landlord is a company, and the landlord must be occupying the property as his main home at the time the tenancy is granted. There are two types of resident landlord situation that now apply:

1. Where the landlord shares accommodation with a licensee (i.e. lodgers).

2. Where the tenant occupies self-contained accommodation in the same building provided this is not a purpose-built block of flats. (e.g. if the landlord has converted a large house into flats and lives in one of them).

Resident landlords have the following legal advantages:

Note

If the landlord (or all of them if more than one) ceases to live at the property as his (or their) main home, the resident landlord exceptions will cease to apply.

- The tenant cannot refer the rent to the Rent Assessment Committee.

- The minimum two months notice period as for shortholds does not apply.

- The protection from eviction legislation does not apply (but see chapter 7).

- The statutory succession provisions do not apply (see below).

Other legal matters landlords need to know

Fixed-term and periodic tenancies

Normally a tenancy agreement states that the tenancy is for a specific period of time (e.g. six months). This is known as a *fixed-term tenancy*. However once the fixed term comes to an end, this does not mean that the tenant has to leave. The law will imply that the tenancy continues on the same terms as the fixed-term tenancy, but on a periodic basis; the period being based on how the rent is paid. This is called a *periodic tenancy*. So if the rent is paid monthly it will be a monthly periodic tenancy, if paid weekly it will be a weekly periodic tenancy, and if paid quarterly it will be a quarterly periodic tenancy. The first period will start the day after the fixed term ends. Say this is Monday 1st January. If the tenancy is a weekly periodic one the next period will start on Monday 8th January, and if it is a monthly one the next period will start on 1st February and so on. On the whole it is advisable that the period should be either weekly or monthly. Periodic tenancies can continue indefinitely, until the landlord or tenant do something to bring the tenancy to an end.

Section 20 Notices

Prior to 28th February 1997, it was necessary to serve a special notice (called a 'section 20 notice', because it was required by section 20 of the Housing Act 1988) on a tenant, before a tenancy was created, if you wanted that tenancy to be an AST. This caused many problems for inexperienced landlords, as the notice had to contain certain prescribed information and was invalid if it did not. Once a tenancy had started, it was impossible for it to be converted into an AST, if no section 20 notice had been served or if the notice served was defective. Happily, section 20 notices are no longer necessary for new tenancies as they were made redundant by the Housing Act 1996, which came into force (so far as section 20 notices were concerned) on 28th February 1997. Section 20 notices are still important, however, for tenancies created between 15 January 1989 and 27 February 1997.

Guarantees

If a landlord is uncertain whether a tenant will be able to pay the rent, he can take security in the form of a guarantee. This is where someone else signs an agreement to confirm that he will pay the rent and any money due from the tenant, if the tenant defaults on his payments. For example, guarantees are normally taken from students' parents in student lets. If the student then leaves the property owing rent, the landlord can sue the guarantor for the student's rent arrears. A guarantee can either be included in the tenancy agreement itself which the guarantor will sign as well as the tenants, or there can be a separate guarantee deed.

Joint and several liability

Where more than one tenant has signed a tenancy agreement, then the general rule is that they will all be 'jointly and severally' liable for the rent. For example, say four students (Matthew, Mark, Luke and John) are renting a house together and they all sign the same tenancy agreement for a total rent of £400 per month. They will no doubt have agreed between themselves that they will each pay £100 per month. However if one of the four tenants, Mark, then stops paying his share (for example if he leaves the house) the landlord is entitled to claim the outstanding rent from any of the tenants, not just from Mark. The landlord is not bound by the tenants' own agreement to pay £100 each. So if one of the tenants, say John, is wealthy, the landlord can sue just John, and get a judgment against him for the outstanding rent, even though he has paid his share.

Also, if the landlord has taken a guarantee from the student's parents (as is often done in student lets), he can normally claim the whole of any outstanding rent from any one parent guarantor, as the parent will effectively be guaranteeing the whole of the rent, not just his son's share.

Letting your own home

If you have lived or are going to live in the property as your main residence, you have an additional mandatory ground for possession available. Provided you give the tenants notice that you may recover possession under this ground (which can be done in the tenancy agreement – see chapter 5), the tenancy does not have to be a shorthold one. This may be advantageous as assured (non-shorthold) tenants cannot challenge the rent in the first six months of the tenancy as shorthold tenants can, and you can, technically, recover possession during the first six months of the tenancy. To obtain these benefits you will have to prevent the tenancy becoming shorthold, which you do by giving notice to the tenant. Please note, however, that you should be absolutely sure before doing this that you will be able to rely on this ground (known as Ground 1), otherwise you may not be able to recover possession of your property. Obtaining possession of a property and the legal grounds for doing so are discussed more detail in chapter 7.

Premiums

This is the term used where a sum of money is paid for a lease or tenancy. It is common practice with long leases. However, as regards short-term tenancies, they were specifically forbidden in the Rent Act 1977. They are not illegal for ATs and ASTs now, provided there is no absolute prohibition against assigning or sub-letting in the tenancy agreement. But this is inadvisable as a landlord of a short term tenancy will want to have control over who occupies the property. Premiums therefore should be avoided.

Succession rights

Having a tenancy is a property right, like owning a house or a flat on a long lease. If a tenant dies, his tenancy does not usually die with him. If a tenancy is a joint one (i.e. if more than one person has signed the tenancy agreement) then it will become the sole property of the remaining tenant. On the death of a sole tenant, provided the tenancy is one carrying succession rights, it will generally pass either to the spouse, or under the tenant's will, or under the intestacy rules (further information is given in chapter 8). It is beyond the scope of this book to go into the succession rules in any detail; if they are relevant to you, you should take legal advice.

Eviction of tenants and eviction notices

The eviction procedure and the various notices (Section 21 – Notices Requiring Possession, and Section 8 – Notices Seeking Possession) are discussed in chapter 8.

Generally

Please note that this book is not intended to be a comprehensive legal textbook, more a general introduction and guide. Many legal points which relate to comparatively few properties or which are unlikely to be relevant to the average private residential landlord are not discussed in this book at all. For a more comprehensive legal coverage, landlords are advised to consult one of the other books available, such as the excellent 'Which Guide to Renting and Letting'. Alternatively, for specific problems, landlords should take legal advice e.g. from a solicitor.

Initial considerations 2

A lot of careful thought is required before letting a property or acquiring a property to let. Different considerations will apply, depending on the type of property you wish to let and the reasons for letting. For example:

- **Your own home.** There are two main reasons why people let their own homes:(1) they are going abroad for a period and will require it on their return and (2) they are unable to sell their property due to negative equity. If you intend living in the property again yourself, you will want to be particularly careful with your choice of tenant, especially if your own furniture is left in the property.

- **Your second home.** You may have a second home which you wish to rent out as a holiday home to earn an income for the periods when you do not wish to stay in it yourself. As you will not, in the nature of things, have your main home local to the property, it is probably best to consider using one of the specialist holiday country cottage letting agencies, at least to start with.

- **Inheritance.** You may have inherited a property, perhaps on the death of your parents, and be considering letting it for an income, rather than selling it. You have slightly more flexibility here as if the property is unsuitable for letting you can sell it and buy another more viable property with the proceeds of sale.

- **Buy to let.** You may be considering purchasing an investment property specifically for letting. See the section below for further details of this.

'Location, location, location' ———————

When letting a property its location is all important. On this will depend the type of tenant you are likely to attract and the level of rent you will be able to achieve. For example, two take identical properties:

1. One is in a popular residential area in a county town, positioned halfway between the university and the centre. This property will be very easy to let and should achieve an above average rent (provided it is in good condition).

2. The other is in a run down part of a large 'inner city' area, with high unemployment. This property will probably be very difficult to let unless you are prepared to take housing benefit tenants. Even then, particularly if the property is in an insalubrious part of town, you may find it impossible to let the property at all.

Even within a comparatively small area, conditions may change. A landlord of a property only a few miles from property 1 above, may find it harder to let or be unable to achieve such a good rent.

Also, conditions change over time. When letting student accommodation for example, it is important that the property is available in June/July when most students are looking to take on a tenancy for the following academic year. Also rents may increase in the short term if a company in the area is looking to re-locate a large number of staff who are all looking for rented accommodation.

The location of a property will also, to a large extent, determine the type of tenancy you will have. For example:

A landlord says ...

'If it is not good enough for you, it is probably not good enough for anyone else to live in.'

- **'Good' areas.** These will be suitable for high-class ASTs. These are usually the most trouble-free tenancies, as you can attract good quality tenants who will look after the property and pay promptly. Your initial investment, however, will be greater as the purchase price will probably be high and tenants will expect the property to be in good condition, with good quality fixtures and fittings.

- **Country properties.** Normally the most suitable type of letting here will be holiday lets. These can be remunerative, particularly if the property is attractive, and in beautiful countryside with local holiday attractions. Again, your investment may be high as holiday makers expect a high standard of comfort and facilities nowadays. Also you may find that some items may need replacing frequently if holidaymakers walk off with them.

- **Inner cities.** This is the type of area where you will find more HMOs and Housing Benefit tenants. These types of lettings are more time-consuming (particularly the HMOs) and you will probably have more problem tenants. However, with the right property and a careful choice of tenant, landlords can do well.

Other considerations

What is your intended type of tenant?

Different types of tenant will be attracted to different types of property. You should do some research into the market and decide what sector you will aim at, for example, students, contract staff, Housing Benefit tenants. Some areas of the market are more profitable and some more labour-intensive. All will have different requirements which need to be borne in mind when purchasing a property and preparing it for letting.

Building or other work

The property as it stands may be unsuitable for letting, or for letting to the type of tenant you are seeking. For example, extensive alterations may be necessary if you intend the property to be an HMO. You should cost very carefully the building work necessary, and any on-going costs, making sure that you have considered all the legal requirements that landlords are subject to, for example, his responsibilities to keep the property in repair (see chapter 3). Bear in mind also that a property let to tenants will generally need more redecoration and other work, than your own home. If there is likely to be a rapid turn-around of tenants, you may well find that you are having to redecorate at least part of the property before every new, or every alternate new letting, if you wish to attract good quality tenants. If the cost is going to render the project economically unviable, it is better to find this out now than after the work has been done.

Fixtures and fittings/furniture

Again, you need to consider the cost of fitting the property for letting, bearing in mind the product safety regulations discussed in chapter 3. Quality tenants will expect good quality fittings and 'white' goods (e.g. fridges, washing machines and cookers) in the property as standard, and will want furniture that is comfortable and attractive. Ensure that your budget is sufficient to provide for this.

A landlord says …

'I always ask myself "Who is going to live in the property and if I were them what would I want"?'

The availability of grants

Often local authority grants are available for improvement work on properties to be let. The availability of grants will vary from authority to authority and from time to time. You should speak to your local authority at the outset to see what is available. The type of grants that may be available include grants for property improvement/repairs, insulation, energy efficiency works, and for fire prevention works. Grants are normally awarded on an annual basis. If you are not successful one year, try again the next!

A landlord says …

'A ropy property in an area the Local Authority wants smartening up will usually get a grant.'

Remember that if you do get a grant, you may have to pay at least part of it back if you sell the property within five years.

Furnished or unfurnished?

For some types of letting you will have no choice: for example students will not want unfurnished properties. Properties let unfurnished are more suitable for longer lets: for example to families who have their own furniture, and will generally achieve a lower rent. You will obtain a higher rent from furnished properties, especially if you are letting to professional people who require short-term accommodation because of work-related moves.

Achievable rent/financial considerations

Be realistic when considering rent. A property marketed at too high a rent is unlikely to find a tenant. When budgeting at this stage, it would be wise to allow for a slightly lower rent than you actually expect to achieve. Also bear in mind that your actual earnings will be less than the monthly rent, even taking into account regular expenses such as mortgage payments. All rented properties will be empty for a period of time between tenants; also you will have maintenance costs, agency fees (if you are letting via an agency), and probably other fees as well.

Tenant default

Always remember that even the best tenants can fall on hard times and can default on their rent. This may result in you having to evict them which will mean legal expenses and a period without rent (as tenants rarely pay rent if they are being evicted). The likelihood of tenant default is far more likely in lower-quality HMOs, but can occur in any type of property. Although tenant default is less likely in better quality lettings, when it does occur it will usually be more expensive – you are more likely to need a possession order and of course the rental you are losing is higher.

On the whole, most tenants are satisfactory. However, every landlord who lets for any period of time will have a bad tenant from time to time, and probably at least one tenant who will need evicting. Remember that 'sod's law' applies to residential letting as it does to every other area of life, and you will probably have your bad experience (if you have one) at the worst possible time. Try to guard against this and keep a special fund to pay for expenses should this type of thing happen.

A landlord says ...

'I always budget on the basis that the property will only be let for 10 months in the year.'

Buy-to-let

Buy-to-let is becoming increasingly popular and it is common to see advertisements for mortgages specifically for investment properties in the residential letting field. Many of these buy-to-let mortgage schemes are very good, and it is certainly worth considering using them to purchase a property for residential letting if you wish to invest, but do not have enough funds to buy outright. But the exercise should be carefully costed, particularly if the mortgage will be for a high percentage of the equity of the property.

When purchasing a property to let you need first to consider 'What is my overall investment objective?' For example:

- You may be looking to purchase a house for your son while he is at university (a common arrangement is for the property to be let to the son and, say, three friends, the friends paying rent and the son living rent-free). This is a short-term objective, i.e. to provide accommodation for him for a limited period (normally three years) and then to sell the property, hopefully at a profit to reimburse you for the maintenance costs of supporting your son.

- Alternatively you may be looking for an income to supplement a pension. This is a long-term objective.

What type of property should you purchase? There are three things to consider:

1. Your investment objective.

2. Whether you want rental income or capital growth as a priority. For example, if you have a good job you may be looking for capital investment, whereas if you are retired you may want to live on the income.

3. Can you visualise a situation where you will want to sell the property quickly? If your answer is yes, then you should look at properties in a prime location, as location sells. Do not look at good rental properties which will be difficult to sell.

You should note the following points:

- Do not buy in a poor location just to get in on the property market. What if you cannot let and cannot sell?

- Beware properties with structural faults. They may show a good rental return but may be impossible to sell. Leave these for the professional investors.

- Flats on long leases – these can be a good investment if you get the right one. However, there are many rogue landlords and poorly drafted leases, so be careful.

- Be very wary indeed of very cheap properties, particularly in poor and run-down areas. You may be taking on a liability rather than an investment.

- Buy new properties rather than old, preferably with small gardens – they will generally need less maintenance.

- Go for smaller properties (not more than two to three bedrooms); they will be easier to market and let than larger ones.

- Take proper advice, particularly if you are on a limited income.

Buying properties with existing tenants

If you are buying a property which is already tenanted, you should check very carefully the status of the existing tenancies. It may be wise to choose a solicitor who has some knowledge of residential lettings to do your conveyancing, rather than a cut-price firm where conveyancing is done on a 'conveyor belt' basis by unqualified staff. The following points are important:

- Establish the date when each tenancy **first** started.

- Try to obtain a copy of the initial tenancy agreement as well as the most recent one (if there has been more than one).

- If the tenancy began between 15 January 1989 and 28 February 1997, make sure that a section 20 notice (explained in chapter 1) was served on the tenant and that you have a copy of the notice that was served and evidence that it was served prior to the tenancy being entered into (as otherwise you will not be able to evict the tenant under the shorthold ground). Ideally you should have a statutory declaration from the person who served the notice on the tenant which exhibits a copy of the notice served.

- If the tenant first went into the property before 15 January 1989, then he will be a Rent Act tenant and you will find it very difficult, if not impossible, to evict him, should this become necessary. Also you will not be able to charge more than the registered 'fair rent' which may be lower than the current market rent.

- Beware if there is no documentation regarding the tenancy.

Houses in multiple occupation

The legal definition of an HMO is a house which is occupied by 'persons who do not form a single household'. However, at the time of writing, the interpretation of this phrase varies between local authorities and the courts and across the country. The government is currently undertaking a review of HMOs and there may be changes in the legislation.

It is generally anticipated that new regulations will require all HMOs to be licensed. At present this depends on the local authority. It is also anticipated that the test for HMOs will be finalised and that there will be severe penalties for landlords who break the new regulations. Landlords of HMOs should therefore keep themselves informed of any new legal developments – the easiest way to do this is by joining a landlord's association.

HMOs need a lot of management and are probably best managed by the landlord rather than a letting agent. Landlords should visit properties at least once a week. A week is a long time in an HMO, particularly where there are many tenants. One bad tenant can affect the whole household, and the landlord has a duty of care to other tenants. A landlord of a HMO needs to know what is going on in his property.

An HMO is subject to more regulations than a normal tenancy. These regulations are largely concerned about the risk involved where people who do not know each other live in close proximity. Also HMO tenants tend to be more transitory and there is often a more rapid turnover. People do not usually stay in an HMO on a long-term basis by choice. There are different categories of HMO and a local authority will specify standards that need to be adhered to for each category, such as the space needed for each occupier and the size of rooms allowable, heating, ventilation, facilities, fire precautions, and management standards.

In addition to the normal landlord's obligations (discussed in chapter 3), the landlord of a HMO must also do the following:

- Maintain the water supply and drainage, and facilities for heating and hot water in good working order.

- Not interrupt the supply of water, gas, or electricity unreasonably.

- Keep shared facilities (such as baths, sanitary conveniences, sinks, fridges, cookers) clean and in proper working order.

- Make sure that the living accommodation is in a clean condition at the start of each resident's occupation.

- Keep windows and ventilation facilities in good repair and proper working order.

- Take precautions to ensure that the premises are safe.

- Keep all fire escapes and fire precautions in good repair and free from obstruction.

- Keep the common parts of the property such as staircases, passageways, landings and balconies clean, in a good state of repair, and free from obstruction, so as not to block a means of escape in the case of fire or any other emergency.

Tip

Before converting a house to an HMO, a landlord should consult with the Environmental Health Department of their local authority to check that the property is suitable for conversion. A difference of a few inches in a room size can be crucial.

- Maintain any outbuildings and yards that form part of the HMO.

- Provide adequate rubbish bins and ensure that rubbish is removed regularly.

- Ensure a notice is displayed giving the name, address, and telephone number of the manager of the HMO.

- Where there is a local registration scheme, provide the local authority with details of occupiers and any changes in occupancy.

Further details of the landlord's responsibilities are set out in the Housing (Management of Houses in Multiple Occupation) Regulations 1990, available from The Stationery Office.

The HMO regulations are largely policed by the environmental health departments of local authorities. They have extensive powers and if necessary they can take over the management of a HMO or, ultimately, issue a compulsory purchase order. However these draconian powers are not usually used except as a final resort.

Local authorities are sometimes proactive and will inspect HMOs of their own volition. However, more usually they are re-active and will only inspect if an HMO has been drawn to their attention. This can be by neighbours worried about noise and rubbish, other tenants concerned about anti-social behaviour, concerned parents of students, and the like. Once a complaint has been received they have a duty to investigate.

However, although the local authority powers are very large, they normally prefer to help landlords put problems right rather than prosecute. Prosecution will normally only be used as a last resort. If landlords follow their advice they should not have a problem.

Landlord associations

If you are considering renting property, check to see if there is a landlords' association in your area. It may be prepared to give you some initial advice. If you decide to take the plunge and become a landlord, your landlords' association will be invaluable. You will normally, however, have to agree to comply with the association's code of practice as a condition of membership. Benefits of membership generally include:

- Regular meetings where you can hear speakers on subjects of interest to landlords and have an opportunity to speak to other, perhaps more experienced, landlords.

- Information on the latest housing legislation, rules, and good practice.

- Practical advice and information.

- A list of approved suppliers, many of whom will offer discounts to members.

- Competitive property and contents insurance cover for members.

- A regular newsletter.

- The respect which usually flows from being a member of a recognised professional body.

Tip

To find the landlords' association for your area, call the National Federation of Residential Landlords (see Appendix 1).

Your local landlords association may also operate a tenancy deposit scheme – see chapter 5.

Most landlord associations are themselves members of the National Federation of Residential Landlords which negotiates on behalf of private residential landlords with the government and with government departments. By being a member of your local association, you may be able to help influence government decisions affecting the private landlord.

Preparation of the property

3

Before preparing your property for letting, you should first ensure that you are legally entitled to let it to tenants.

Permission for letting

This may be necessary, for example:

- If the property is leasehold, you will need to check your lease carefully. Usually in a long lease you will need your own landlord's permission before sub-letting, or you may have to give notice. You should ensure that any terms in your lease are complied with.

- If there is a mortgage on the property, you will need to obtain the lender's permission to let. This is normally granted, although some lenders will only give consent subject to a small increase in the interest rate on the loan. If you do not obtain the lender's consent, strictly speaking you will be in breach of the mortgage agreement and they may be entitled to call in the loan. Any conditions imposed by the lender should be complied with.

Planning permission

This is not normally necessary unless you are 'developing' a property e.g. converting a single home to an HMO. However, even if you are going to let the property as one unit, if you intend having more than six tenants, you should always check to see if planning permission is needed, as this may constitute a material change of use. Your local planning officer will advise you.

If planning permission is needed (for example if you are converting a property into a number of flats), the planning officer will probably be looking at the availability of parking, so ensure that there is adequate parking at the property. He will also be considering such things as fire prevention, sound proofing, and compliance with the HMO regulations. If you are developing an HMO it is important that you comply with all requirements, as the environmental health department will inevitably find out about the property sooner or later, e.g. from the benefit office when tenants claim benefit. If you do not have planning permission, they will then be serving enforcement notices on you. When planning permission is granted, it is important that you do not exceed the permitted number of tenants.

Remember that if you are carrying out any building works, you will also need to comply with building regulations. You should not confuse building regulations with planning permission; the two are separate and both must be complied with.

Renovations and repairs

Once you have dealt with any preliminary legal requirements, you then need to put the property into a proper condition to let.

It is most important that the property is in a good condition *before* it is let. For example:

- Cutting costs and not having the property in a good state of repair will not attract good tenants which may result in problems later in the tenancy. Most people are not prepared to put up with poor quality accommodation nowadays.

- You may not have access during the letting.

- If the property is in poor repair you will be vulnerable to claims by the tenants (who may be eligible for Legal Aid) who can apply for an injunction and/or

Tip

Watch out for agricultural restrictions on properties on farms: their use may be limited to occupation by farm workers.

damages, or you may have a repairs notice served on you by the local authority.

- It is easier to ensure that the property is left in a good condition after the tenants leave, if it is in a good condition when they arrive.

- You will have complied with your legal obligations which will make it difficult for tenants to justify any non-compliance with their obligations (such as payment of rent!).

A landlord has a duty to put a property into proper repair before it is let to tenants and to keep it in proper repair once it is let. Under the Landlord and Tenant Act 1985, private residential landlords are responsible for:

- The structure and exterior of the dwelling.

- Installations for the supply of water, gas and electricity and for sanitation.

- Basins, sinks, baths and other sanitary installations.

- Heating and hot water installations.

If you are considering converting a property to an HMO, there will be other standards you will have to comply with and you should consult your local authority before doing any work (see HMO section above).

For major work you may wish to consider employing a qualified architect or surveyor to oversee it. As discussed above, you may be eligible for a Local Authority grant for works, particularly if you are converting a property to an HMO. You will usually need two written estimates of the cost. As always with building works, you need to be careful with your choice of builder. You may wish to consider using one who belongs to a trade association which operates a guarantee scheme such as those run by the Building Employees Confederation or the Federation of Master Builders.

Remember that if a property is in poor condition, the local authority environmental health department may serve a repairs notice on you, and has draconian powers to enforce this if necessary.

Building regulations

Before carrying out any building work, you need to check whether building regulations apply. If they do, you will have to obtain approval of your proposed works before they start and they will have to be inspected after completion. Your architect/surveyor/builder should be able to arrange this for you.

Heating

It will be difficult to let the property unless it has proper heating, and this generally means central heating. Providing proper heating will also mean that tenants are less likely to use their own heating devices, such as gas cylinder heaters, which may be dangerous. It is often a good idea to specify in the tenancy agreement that the heating facilities provided (e.g. central heating) must be used and to prohibit other forms of heating, particularly oil and gas cylinder heaters.

Condensation

This is mentioned here as it is probably the most common complaint about properties nation-wide. It can be avoided by landlords installing proper heating, insulation, and ventilation. However it is sometimes caused by tenants not heating the property and not opening the windows. If this is likely to be a problem, it might be a good idea for the tenancy agreement to provide that the property should be heated to a certain specified level in the winter.

Gas Regulations

The Gas Safety (Installation and Use) Regulations 1998

These are to ensure the safety of all gas appliances in all let properties and must be strictly adhered to. Badly maintained gas appliances can kill. A landlord must:

- Have all gas appliances (including mobile gas heaters) properly installed by a CORGI-registered plumber (see Appendix for details).

- Before a property is let, and annually thereafter, all gas appliances must be checked by a CORGI-registered plumber.

- A copy of the gas certificate stating that a check has been done and detailing any work done must be handed to a tenant at the start of a tenancy and provided to them annually thereafter (within 28 days of the annual check being completed).

- For properties, such as holiday lets, where occupancy is under 28 days, a copy of the safety check record should be posted in a prominent position in the premises.

- A landlord cannot delegate maintenance or safety checks to a tenant.

- All gas certificates *must* be kept for at least two years, but landlords are advised to keep them for at least six years, just in case they are needed as evidence in any claim brought in respect of the property.

Remember, the landlord is ultimately responsible for the safety of all gas appliances in properties let by him. This means that if a tenant dies of carbon monoxide poisoning, he is the one who will be prosecuted for manslaughter. The only way you can protect against this happening to you is to ensure that comprehensive checks are carried out each year by a CORGI-registered plumber who is authorised to do the work, and to ensure that all complaints received from the tenant are dealt with immediately. Keep proper records of everything so you can prove, if necessary, that you have complied with the law.

The regulations are administered by the Health and Safety Executive, which is also the enforcing body. Breach of the regulations is a criminal offence punishable either by a fine of up to £5,000 for each offence, or an unlimited fine/imprisonment if the case is referred to the Crown Court.

Problems to watch out for:

- Dust and detritus in a gas appliance which can cause it to become unsafe. A sign of this is when the colour of the flame changes to a smoky yellow.

Tip

Landlords should obtain the Health & Safety Executive Code of Practice and Guidance, which sets out the Regulations and advises how they can best be complied with. The obligations of landlords are summarised in a leaflet called 'A Guide to Landlords' Duties' available free from HSE Books (see Appendix 1).

- Black soot deposits around gas appliances.

- Cracks in the cement blocks found in older fires and mobile heaters.

- Poor ventilation, caused either by a blocked flue or ventilation in a room (e.g. air bricks) becoming blocked, which can cause a build-up of carbon monoxide in the air.

- Gas leaks, e.g. if gas pipes become damaged. It is important to ensure that vulnerable pipes are protected.

Tip

For further advice about gas safety issues landlords can ring the HSE Gas Safety Advice Line (see Appendix 1).

Electricity

At the time of writing there are no specific regulations requiring certification for electrical installations in rented property. However, the landlord has a general duty to provide a safe environment and is strongly advised to have the electrical installations regularly checked. Remember that a common cause of fire is faulty electrical installations and the landlord can be found liable to the tenant for any losses. You will generally be protected from claims by tenants if you have the property inspected before the tenants go in, and deal with all complaints promptly.

If you intend to let to students, a students' union will generally require all properties on their list to have an annual inspection report covering the electrical installation at the property from an electrical contractor who is a member of the National Inspection Council for Electrical Installation Contractors (NICEIC). Further information can be obtained from your local college students' union.

A landlord says ...

'I was glad I had arranged for an electrical inspection when the Inspector found a live wire in one of the walls, due to unauthorised wall lights having been installed and then removed by the previous tenants.'

Fire safety

This is particularly important for HMOs where there are strict regulations. However, it is important that this is considered for all properties, if only to protect your investment.

You should consider the following points when preparing a property for letting:

- Try to protect the staircase, so that everyone can get out in an emergency, by fitting self-closing doors to all rooms.

- Fit smoke detectors to give warning in the event of a fire. For HMOs, these need to be interlinked mains-powered smoke detectors. For large HMOs, the smoke alarms need to be linked to a commercial fire alarm system.

- It should be possible for the front door to be opened at all times from the inside. Cylinder locks are better here than mortice locks which need to be unlocked with a key. If you feel a mortice lock is essential, get one with a thumb turn from the inside. Also possible but less satisfactory (because it can get lost or be stolen) is to have a spare key hanging by the door.

- Give new tenants an information pack regarding fire safety in the property.

- Place notices in HMOs showing exit routes in the case of fire, and the location of the nearest phone for calling the fire brigade.

- Consider having a fire blanket and a small dry powder extinguisher in the kitchen (but if the property is an HMO discuss this with the fire officer).

- Try to make escape routes (e.g. passages and corridors) 'fire sterile', i.e. do not have anything that can burn on the walls – use emulsion paint rather than wallpaper or hessian covering.

For larger HMOs you should also consider:

- Emergency lighting (this may be mandatory for some local authorities).

- Arranging means of escape through adjacent buildings.

- Fire-retardant curtains.

Make sure that you take proper advice on fire safety and get the necessary work done before the tenants move in. You should speak first to your local environmental health officer; however, the fire safety department at your local fire brigade will often be pleased to advise.

Water

When converting properties into flats, the water company may have the right to install water meters. There may be problems thereafter with apportionment and payment of water bills if for example two or more flats have a shared water heater. Ideally each flat should have its own water meter. Often, for example in HMOs, the landlord pays the water bills; however, if the water is metered, this may mean large bills for you, as tenants rarely economise on something that is free to them. If they are annoyed with you for any reason they may even leave taps running deliberately.

Fitting out the property

To a certain extent, the standard of fittings and furnishings will depend upon the type of tenant you are catering for. However, generally standards have increased recently and you will find it difficult to find good tenants if the property does not have good quality fittings and furniture. Obviously they should all comply with the product safety regulations described below.

Most people will now require as standard good quality 'white goods' e.g. cookers, fridges, washing machines etc. Furniture should be attractive but hard wearing. Even if you are letting a property unfurnished, it will need to be carpeted and have curtains.

Product safety regulations

These regulations generally apply when a landlord is letting a property as a commercial venture. This includes properties which are being let via an agent. As a matter of good practice, however, the regulations should be complied with in all cases. If a landlord is letting his own home, say while he is working abroad for a year leaving his own furniture in the property, then the regulations will probably not apply.

The various product safety regulations apply to anything supplied as part of a property, but not permanently fixed.

An HMO landlord says …

'If utility bills are in the name of tenants, they will often do a runner when the bills come in. I am not responsible for the bills, but I have all the bother of having to find another tenant.'

A landlord says …

'It is best to use good quality carpeting as cheap carpets stain easily and are often difficult to clean.'

A trading standards officer says …

'If in doubt, chuck it out.'

Furniture and furnishings

The Furniture and Furnishings (Fire) (Safety) Regulations apply to all furniture and soft furnishings which must be fire-safety compliant. Items covered include: padded headboards, sofas, mattresses, pillows, cushions, nursery furniture, and cloth covers on seats. Make sure that all items carry the proper label.

Items which are exempt are furniture made before 1950 (and re-upholstery of furniture made before that date), curtains and carpets, duvets, and sheets.

There is a very helpful guide to the regulations published by the Department of Trade and Industry which can be obtained from your local trading standards office, who will also be able to give you general advice.

Electrical equipment

The Electrical Equipment (Safety) Regulations control the supply of electrical equipment. This covers all electrical goods, i.e. kettles, TVs, fires, fridges, etc., which must be safe. It is best to have them tested by a bona fide qualified electrician, preferably annually. Keep records of all inspections and testing, with lists of the items inspected and details of their condition. Things to watch out for include:

- Plugs, which need to be sleeved.

- Old cookers, as the plates may become live if the insulation is old.

- Bare or damaged wire on leads.

- Small moveable objects which are more likely to be damaged through wear and tear.

General product safety

The General Product Safety Regulations control the supply of general consumer products. These regulations cover general problems in properties such as missing rungs in ladders, step ladders with faulty locking devices, and slippery carpets. Anything supplied in the property needs to be safe.

You need to ensure this, not only because otherwise you might become liable for prosecution under the regulations, but also because you might otherwise become liable for a civil claim for damages, if someone is injured as a result of the unsafe item. You should therefore always ensure that there are no unsafe items when properties are let, and make sure that repairs are done quickly, once they are brought to your attention by your tenant.

The best way to deal with these regulations is to draw up a full inventory of all upholstered furniture, electrical equipment, and general consumer products in the property, and make a note of their general condition. You should then make sure that all of any identified problems are dealt with before the property is let. This should also be done every time the property is vacated before re-letting. Keep records of all checks (e.g. electrical checks) done, repairs, and items replaced. Keep all invoices and receipts (you should also keep these to claim against tax).

The Trading Standards Office is the prosecuting authority for offences under these regulations. However, they will normally want to work with a landlord to put things right and will only prosecute as a last resort. They are always happy to advise and new landlords should contact them at an early stage as they usually have useful advice/fact sheets which landlords will find helpful.

Tip

These regulations do not apply to the tenant's own furniture and possessions. However these must be removed when they leave the property.

Insurance

You need to be sure that your insurance is suitable for rented property. If you are letting your own home, do not rely on your ordinary household insurance. In particular, ensure that your insurer knows that the property is rented. With insurance, you have a duty of good faith to tell the insurer all relevant factors. If you do not, the insurer can refuse to pay when a claim is made.

Even if you are only letting rooms in your own home, you need to check that you are adequately insured.

Insurance for rented properties generally needs to cover the following:

- The structure of the property.

- Landlord's contents, fittings and fixtures (the tenant generally insures his own possessions).

- Public liability – this is to cover you in the event of tenants or members of the general public making a claim in respect of personal injury or death, or damage to their possessions. It is recommended that this should be for a minimum of at least five million pounds. This sounds a lot, but claims from several people, particularly if they are seriously injured, could be extremely expensive.

- Loss of rent following damage to the property.

You might also wish to consider insurance cover for:

- The cost of finding alternative accommodation for your tenants.

- Legal expenses.

- Non-payment of rent (a rent guarantee policy).

If you take out any of these policies it is wise to read the small print, which will usually specify actions that need to be taken before a claim can be made. For example, letters demanding payment of unpaid rent will normally need to be sent to the tenant within a specified period of time. If this is not done, cover may be refused.

If you are considering letting to asylum seekers, Housing Benefit tenants or students be sure to check that the policy does not exclude these. Remember that tenants' circumstances can change, for example they may go on benefit without you knowing about it. However, this would not stop your insurers refusing to pay when a claim is made.

As with all insurance, you also need to insure for the correct sum. If the structure of the property is underinsured, this will affect payouts not only when there is total destruction of the property but also for smaller claims, as insurers will say that you have only insured a proportion of the property. Your surveyor will be able to advise you of the current rebuilding costs.

Most landlords' associations will have a special insurance policy available for members and this is usually excellent value. If this is not available, you should consult an independent insurance broker for advice before taking out insurance.

Rent

If you are a new landlord, it may be best to take professional advice when setting rent levels for the first time. Multiple occupancy (e.g. renting individual rooms in a property, to students say, on separate agreements) will often achieve a higher rent than letting the property as a whole, certainly if you are letting to tenants on Housing Benefit this will normally be the case. Sources of information for local rental levels include: properties let by other agents, local papers, and the internet e.g. landlord association web-sites.

The rental market is different from the selling market. Rental levels can fluctuate more from one month to the next and from one area to another.

If you are including Council Tax and any utilities in the rent (as will often be the case with HMOs), you should, particularly if the property is being let to tenants on Housing Benefit, apportion the rent between pure rental and payment for each individual service or tax. Your tenancy agreement should make provision for the rent to increase in line with services or Council Tax.

A letting agent says …

'We have a saying, **"The greedy man goes hungry"**. Do not market at too high a price. Consider the difference between your losses with an empty property at a silly asking rent and your profits with a property let at a moderate rent. Remember if the property is standing empty you will still have outgoings to pay.'

Finding a tenant

4

Letting agents

If the landlord is not local to the property, there is usually no alternative to using a letting agent. It is essential that there is someone local to the property that the tenant can contact if there is a problem, and who can keep an eye on it and inspect it regularly. Even if the landlord does live locally, he may not have sufficient time to manage the property properly, in which case it is best to use an agent. However, if the landlord can manage the property himself the financial returns will be higher, as he will not have to pay the agent's commission. HMOs are best managed by the landlord personally as letting agents are rarely able to give the degree of supervision that an HMO property requires.

Agents will charge a fee and this will usually be by way of a commission. They normally offer two types of service. One of these will be an introduction service where they find a tenant and the landlord manages the property thereafter. Their commission here will usually be in the region one month's rent. Normally, however, they will prefer landlords to use their full management service. Here their fees will be in the region of 10–15 per cent of rents collected. Usually agents will also charge extra for providing an inventory, tenancy agreements, overseas telephone calls, and other special services. The cheapest agent is not necessarily the best – the fact that they are cheap may mean that they are unqualified, give staff no training, and don't pay professional association subscription fees.

When choosing an agent, it is best to choose one which is a member of a professional association such as the Association of Residential Letting Agents (ARLA) or the Royal Institute of Chartered Surveyors (RICS), where you can expect a high standard of professional competence, a knowledge of the regulations, and fidelity bonding (a client money protection scheme).

All other things being equal, it is wise to choose an agent who has been in the area a long time. They will usually have a greater depth of knowledge, and local knowledge is very important in this field.

A careful choice of agent is very important, particularly if you are going to be living abroad, as it is not unknown for agents to go out of business, which normally means that the landlord loses rent paid to the agent but not yet paid to him, and the deposit (if there is no client's money protection scheme). This can put the landlord in financial difficulties if, for example, there are payments, such as mortgage payments, which need to paid on the property, and he will be responsible for returning the deposit to the tenant. Also the landlord will have to take over the management of the tenancy at what might be an extremely inconvenient moment.

A letting agent will almost invariably ask you to sign a management contract. Make sure that this specifies that the agent will be responsible for carrying out the maintenance and safety check duties (e.g. regarding the Gas Regulations), and for keeping all associated records. The agent will also need authorisation to spend up to a specified sum on general repairs and maintenance.

Letting agents can also deal with the preliminary aspects of evicting tenants (should this be necessary), such as writing letters and serving notices; but a solicitor will have to be instructed for any court proceedings. The agent can deal with this on your behalf if you wish, but the solicitor will need to see either a written authority from you confirming that the agent can give instructions on your behalf, or a power of attorney.

If you are going to be resident abroad, it is usually a good idea in any case to arrange for someone to have a power of attorney (either the letting agent, your solicitor, or a relative or trusted friend) so that if a problem arises while you are unavailable, someone is empowered to deal with it. However, unless you have absolute faith in that person, it is a good idea for the power of attorney to be limited (e.g. so they cannot sell the property and disappear with the proceeds!). A solicitor will be able to advise you and draft the power of attorney for you or see the Law Pack *Powers of Attorney & Living Will Guide.*

Advertising for tenants

The following are some of the most common methods:

- **Newspapers and magazines.** You should choose the paper most likely to be read by your target class of tenant. Usually this will be the local paper. Most local papers will have a particular day in the week when local property is advertised, and may have a property supplement. However, sometimes a different paper may be appropriate. For example, holiday cottages are often advertised in the Sunday papers or in glossy magazines. If your tenants generally come from a particular large company in your area, they may have an in-house journal where you can advertise.

- **Shop windows.** This can be a cheap way of advertising a property if you are looking for a local tenant. Most newsagent shops offer this service.

- **Notice boards.** Perhaps the best example of this is university notice boards, if you wish to advertise properties for students. Be warned, however, that many student unions will only allow landlords who meet certain (often stringent) quality standards to advertise. Local businesses may, if you provide accommodation regularly for their staff, allow you to put a card on their notice board.

- **The Internet.** This is an up-and-coming method of advertising properties. It is a very good way of advertising properties to students as they almost always have free internet access via their university library. Landlord associations often have a web-site where members can advertise their properties, or if you are a large landlord, you could consider setting up your own web-site. As time goes by, this will probably become one of the most important methods of advertising properties, both to rent and to sell.

The Property Misdescriptions Act 1991

It is not often realised that this Act can apply to advertising rented properties. This is when properties are being let by letting agents and by anyone carrying on a 'property development business'. This includes anyone who refurbishes a building with a view to letting it for profit. The Act provides that criminal sanctions are available against these persons making untrue statements about properties.

It is therefore important that all statements you make about the property are true, both in your advertising and when you discuss the property with prospective tenants. As well as the criminal sanctions under the Act, if untruthful statements are made, the tenant may be entitled to cancel the tenancy agreement and claim back any money paid, under a legal rule known as 'misrepresentation'.

Paramount importance of a good tenant

Finding a good tenant is the single most important thing in letting a property (and good tenants can be worth a lot of money). If you have a good tenant, then any problems can be dealt with comparatively easily as the tenant will be reasonable about them (provided of course that you are, too). If you have a bad tenant you will have nothing but trouble and may even end up out of pocket.

For example :

A landlord lets to a 'hippie'-type family as he is anxious to have tenants in his empty property and the family say that they are desperate for accommodation. He is not entirely happy about them but feels that letting them in will be better than leaving the property empty. Once in, they proceed to redecorate the property, painting the walls black and all the radiators dark mauve. Numerous complaints are received from neighbours about their behaviour and loud music at night. There are several incidents when the police are called out and it is suspected that they are taking drugs. They pay one month's rent in advance but fail to pay any rent thereafter, and the landlord has to issue proceedings for possession to evict them. This process takes four months, by which time the rent arrears have risen to several thousand pounds. The night before the bailiff is due to come to evict them, they have a party, during the course of which several windows are broken, and other damage is done to the property. It is left in a filthy state with rubbish in all the rooms. Much of the furniture has been either broken or stolen. The landlord is left with a property which needs several thousand pounds' work (including redecoration throughout and replacement of almost all the furniture) to make it fit for re-letting, a bill from his solicitors for the eviction proceedings, and no chance of recovery from the tenants who have disappeared without trace.

This scenario is fictitious but all of the individual elements are drawn from the writer's own experience as a solicitor involved in evicting tenants. An experience as dire as this is rare; however this does not mean that it will not ever happen to you. Be careful whom you let into your property. Once in, it is difficult and time consuming to get tenants out, and there is little you can do, physically, to stop them damaging your property while they are in occupation.

By and large, there are many more good tenants 'out there' than bad. You need to develop techniques to ensure that the bad tenants in your properties are kept to a minimum.

Ideally, you will be looking for a tenant with a permanent job who will look after the property and will want to stay there a long time. Long-term lets are preferable because this reduces the costs of letting and periods of time when the property is empty (when you will not be receiving rent).

References

The main types of references are employer's, bank, previous landlords, and character references.

The employer's reference is the most important as it gives some assurance that the tenant will be able to pay the rent. Remember that the applicant's current landlord's reference may not tell the whole picture if the landlord is anxious for the tenant to leave,

A landlord says …

'It is better to have a good tenant paying £300 per month than a bad tenant paying £350.'

and character references can be unreliable (beware the reference which is too glowing – it is probably fictitious).

You should look for tenants with a good employment history. If the tenant has had frequent job changes in the past, this trend will probably continue, and he is less likely to stay in the property for any length of time.

References are particularly important for the more expensive properties, where they should be taken as a matter of course. However, for HMOs, many landlords do not take references and go by their own judgment. HMO tenants are usually in a hurry and are not prepared to wait for the time it would take for the landlord to obtain a reference. If there is any delay, they may well go elsewhere.

Credit rating agencies

These are usually fairly cheap and very useful: for example they will pick up on the tenant who has county court judgments registered against them. Your landlords' association will usually be able to suggest a suitable company.

'Gut' feeling

This is often the best way of deciding whether a tenant will be suitable or not. It is a skill which develops with experience. Every landlord will have their own idiosyncrasies, and preferences and prejudices when choosing tenants. There follow some comments from experienced landlords on how they chose their tenants.

> Never let a property to someone who comes to you desperate for immediate accommodation, particularly if it is late at night. These people will almost always turn out to be nightmare tenants.

> A person with a cheerful, friendly disposition, and who has a sense of humour is more likely to be a good tenant than someone who is grumpy and miserable.

> Do not be prejudiced against Housing Benefit tenants. It is more important to consider the type of person they are.

Comments from HMO landlords:

> I never let to a tenant who is bigger and meaner looking than me.

A landlord says ...

'Do not trust fulsome character references – they are usually untrue.'

A landlord says ...

'If in doubt, keep them out.'

Beware of the tenant who, when you ask him where he is living at the moment, says 'I am staying round a mates'.

If people do not tell you where they are coming from or give you any personal information, don't let them in. There is almost always a problem past.

I have generally found that foreigners and people from ethnic minorities make very good tenants. They are more respectful than many English people and usually would not dream of leaving a flat in a mess.

Do not be prejudiced against a tenant's looks. Be aware of different cultures and age groups. Remember, con men are always well dressed and appear respectable.

Choosing a good tenant is particularly important for high-rental properties, as the inevitable delay in obtaining an eviction order may result in large losses. If a landlord is uncertain about the tenant's ability to pay the rent, he should take security in the form of a guarantee. However, careful checks should also be carried out against the guarantor, as there is no point in taking a guarantee from someone unless they are financially in a position to make good any losses caused by the tenant.

Housing Benefit tenants

If a tenant is on benefit, he may be entitled to have all or part of his rent paid by Housing Benefit. There are many problems associated with Housing Benefit and many landlords have a policy of not letting to Housing Benefit tenants, although in some localities landlords will have little choice. However, provided you are careful when selecting tenants, they can be profitable and problem-free.

When a new Housing Benefit tenant is taken on, there is much that the landlord can do to help speed up the process. Housing Benefit offices are often accused of unwarranted delays; however these are frequently because they are still missing some of the information they need before the application can be processed. It is important for your cash flow that payment is made to you as quickly as possible. Also, if there are long delays resulting in a large sum being sent to the tenant at a later stage, there is a great temptation for the tenant to spend this (rather than give it to you). The following points will help you:

Note

It is often possible to let property on a long term basis to companies for housing asylum seekers. If you are interested in this you can obtain further information from your local landlords' association.

Tip

When doing a company let, check that it is a genuine company. You can do a basic company search for free on the Companies House web-site (see Appendix).

- The application should go in well before the tenant is due to move into the property. Housing Benefit cannot normally be backdated to before an application is made.

- Under the verification framework, Housing Benefit officers will need to see original documents. In particular they will need to see the original tenancy agreement. Ensure that these are sent to the Housing Benefit office promptly.

- Tenants should be asked to sign a letter of authority (see sample letter opposite) authorising the Housing Benefit office to provide information to the landlord. If this is not done, the Housing Benefit officers will not be able to give any information to the landlord about the progress of the tenant's application, even if they want to.

- If you regularly let to Housing Benefit tenants, you may wish to consider keeping a stock of the claim forms to give them.

- Some tenants, particularly those who find writing difficult or whose first language is not English, may appreciate your help in filling in the application form. If you do this, you will at least have the security of knowing that the form has actually been completed and submitted! Remember that if you fill in the form for the tenant, you have to state on the form that you have done this.

- The form asks that where the rent includes services (such as water rates, heating, and cleaning), it should be stated how much of the rent figure is in respect of each of these. There are government guidelines as to how much can be paid (if anything) in respect of each type of service. However, if the Benefit Office is provided with suitable original evidence, they might be able to depart from these guidelines. If you are able to assist your tenant by providing this information, this will help speed up his application considerably.

Sample tenant's letter of authority to Housing Benefit office

[Prospective tenant's name]
[Prospective tenant's address]

To :
The Housing Benefit Office
[address of local office]

Dear Sirs

Re: [address of property to be let]

I hereby authorise and request you to provide my landlord [name of landlord] at [address of landlord] any information s/he may request regarding my application for Housing Benefit and any other information s/he may request regarding my Housing Benefit entitlement and payment of Housing Benefit to me after my application has been processed. I also authorise you to provide details of previous applications for Housing Benefit if these are going to affect the rent paid to my current landlord.

*I hereby request that Housing Benefit is paid direct to my landlord at [landlord's address].

Yours faithfully

Signed .... Dated ....
          [FULL NAME OF TENANT]

(*Delete if you do not want benefit paid direct to you)

- If your property is an HMO, make sure that each individual unit can be identified, e.g. by giving a room number. Try not to change these numbers as otherwise this can cause problems at the Housing Benefit office and may cause them to stop payment of the benefit, if the change makes it appear as if the same room is being claimed for twice.

- Remember that Housing Benefit will be limited to the allowable rent for a unit of a suitable size for the applicant. For example, a single parent with a child needs a two-bedroomed property. If he claims in respect of a three-bedroomed property, he will normally only receive Housing Benefit to the value of a two-bedroomed property and will have to find the difference himself. This situation may lead to arrears building up. This should be borne in mind when renting to Housing Benefit tenants.

- It is possible for tenants to apply to the Rent Officer and ask him to advise in advance the rent figure that will be used as a starting point for working out their Housing Benefit entitlement.

All applications for Housing Benefit for private rented properties are referred to a rent officer for determination. This is described in the separate section on the Rent Service, see below.

Housing Benefit claw-back

One of the advantages of letting to Housing Benefit tenants is that their rent can be paid to you direct by the Housing Benefit office. This means that you get paid regularly and the tenant is not tempted to spend his rent cheque on other things. However, one potential problem with this is that if the Housing Benefit office discovers that an overpayment of benefit has been made to a previous landlord of the tenant, even in respect of a completely different property in another part of the country, it can deduct the overpayment from rent paid to the current landlord. It is difficult for a landlord to prevent this happening as, strictly speaking, the Housing Benefit is a benefit due to the tenant, not the landlord, whose contractual relationship is with the tenant, not the Housing Benefit office, although the payment can be made direct to the landlord. There are several things landlords can do to protect themselves from Housing Benefit claw-back:

- Check all new Housing Benefit tenants very careful-ly and take a reference from their previous landlord. This sort of problem is more likely to occur with the less 'respectable' type of tenants, particularly if they move frequently from one property to another.

- Visit the property regularly so you can advise the Benefit office if the tenant has vacated or if there are any other changes in their circumstances that affect their benefit (so there will not be an overpayment to you).

- If you are concerned that there may have been a pre-vious overpayment to the tenant, insist that the rent is paid to you by the tenant, rather than paid directly to you by the Benefit office. The Benefit office can only claw back from the landlord rent that has been paid to the landlord direct.

- Join your local landlords' association. Sometimes they have a protocol agreement regarding the cir-cumstances in which a claw-back can be recovered from a landlord.

- If a claim is made against you for a claw-back, check that any paperwork served on you by the Benefit office requesting a repayment is correct (if it is not they may not be entitled to repayment). Your local landlords' association will be able to advise you here.

Tip

Ensure that the letter of authority which the tenant signs authorises the Benefit office to discuss previous benefit claims with you, as well as their current claim.

Generally

Try to keep on good terms with your local Housing Benefit office, particularly if you have several tenants who are on bene-fit. If you are considerate and helpful towards them, they are more likely to reciprocate. Remember also that the landlord has a duty to the Benefit office, if rent is being paid direct, to keep them informed, in particular if the tenant vacates the property or is absent for a long period. You should also let them know if you become aware of any other circumstances which may affect their benefit, such as the birth of a child, someone else moving into the property, or the tenant getting a job.

The Rent Service and the assessment of rent for Housing Benefit

This service (formerly the Rent Officer Service) was started in 1965. It was originally administered by the Department of the Environment (now Department of the Environment, Transport and the Regions (DETR)) via a 'Proper Officer' scheme delegated to local authorities, but is now a nationally managed service and an agency of the DETR, Transport and the Regions. It is independent of ministers and local government and is an information service which aims to be unbiased, transparent, and consistent.

The service has a huge database of market rents which is regularly updated from information provided by private landlords, letting agencies and other sources. Its main tasks are:

- To determine average rents based on size of accommodation and locality.

- To advise Housing Benefit officers on the rent charged to tenants claiming Housing Benefit.

- To make 'fair rent' valuations for Rent Act tenancies.

- To advise local authorities about the effects on rent of housing renovation grant applications by landlords.

- To provide advice generally and information for national statistics.

Periodically, the rent officer will determine the local reference rent ('LRR') for eight categories of accommodation in the different localities within his area. He will also, on a monthly basis, provide the local authority with indicative rent levels ('IRL') for these categories of accommodation for the local authority area. The difference between LRR and IRL is that the LRR areas are not restricted by local authority boundaries. The eight categories of property are:

1. A room where a substantial proportion of the rent is attributable to board and/or attendance.

2. A room, e.g. a bedsit with or without some services.

3.   A room with its own facilities such as a studio flat or a bedsit.

4.   A two-roomed property.

5.   A three-roomed property.

6.   A four-roomed property.

7.   A five-roomed property.

8.   A six- or more roomed property.

For the purpose of these categories, 'room' only includes bedrooms and living rooms (i.e. not kitchens or bathrooms). The properties can be any type of accommodation (i.e. houses, flats, etc).

When a rent is referred to the rent officer for valuation he will have to consider:

•   Is the property worth the rent being charged in comparison to similar properties where Housing Benefit is not being claimed?

•   Is the property the appropriate size for the tenants?

•   What is the appropriate LRR for a property of this category?

•   If the property exceeds the size criteria for the claimant, what would be an appropriate rent for a property of the appropriate type and size AND what LRR should apply?

The rent officer will then report back to the local authority and advise on the appropriate rent that can be claimed. This is called the 'claimant related rent'.

The Housing Benefit office will only be able to obtain subsidy from the government for the appropriate LRR for the size of property the applicant is entitled to. For example, if the applicant is single and under 25 he will normally only be entitled to the appropriate rent for a property in categories 1–3 (single room rent – SRR). A family with one child will be entitled to the LRR for a three-roomed property (two bedrooms and a living room). Local authorities may decide to pay more than the LRR but they will have to make up the difference from their own resources. For example, they may make a policy decision to do this in the special case of disabled tenants.

The Rent Service is a public service and rent officers are usually prepared to give information to anyone who makes an enquiry about local rent levels in the area, current local reference rents, and any other information that may be helpful. They cannot, however, give specific advice about rent for individual properties.

For more information about the Rent Service you can contact their headquarters in London, telephone number 020 7388 4838. See Appendix 1 for their full address.

The agreement

5

Why and when necessary?

Although it is not strictly necessary to have one to create a valid AST, all landlords should ensure that their tenants have signed a written tenancy agreement prior to going into possession. Informal oral arrangements can be a recipe for disaster:

- If a tenancy is oral, there may be arguments later about its terms, even if these were clearly discussed when the tenant went in.

- Once a tenant is in occupation, you cannot then force him to sign an agreement that varies the terms of his tenancy, so it is essential that this is done before he goes in.

- The landlord will need a formal agreement so he can insert clauses that will protect his position (see below) and regulate the tenant's use of the property.

- It may be difficult to evict the tenant if there is no written tenancy agreement.

- If no written tenancy agreement is provided, a land-lord is required by law to provide the tenant with written details of the main terms of his tenancy with-in six months; so he might as well provide a proper written tenancy agreement to begin with.

However although all *tenancies* should have a formal written tenancy agreement, this is not always essential with *licences*. For example, it may not always be necessary in the following circumstances:

- Letting a room in your house to lodgers.

- Holiday lettings.

- Bed-and-breakfast accommodation.

However, even if a formal letting agreement is not provided, there should always be some paperwork to prove the terms of the letting, in case there is a dispute at a later date.

The Unfair Terms in Consumer Contracts Regulations 1999

These will be referred to in this book as the Unfair Terms Regulations. These regulations are the result of an EU directive which initially came into effect in July 1995; they were subsequently re-drafted and updated regulations came into effect on 1st October 1999.

These regulations apply to all contracts which involve a 'consumer' (i.e. an individual not acting for the purposes of his business or profession) and a 'seller or supplier' (which definition includes all landlords who let property as a business). They were designed to prevent consumers being placed at a disadvantage when signing formal contracts with large organisations, whose contracts normally include standard terms and conditions in small print. As everyone knows, these standard terms and conditions are rarely read by the consumer before signing the contract, and even if they are, he has no power to change them. The regulations provide that the consumer will not be bound by a standard term in such a contract if that term is 'unfair'.

These regulations apply to most tenancy agreements, as a landlord will generally be deemed to be acting in the course of a business. They will not apply to landlords who are simply letting their own home (for example during a year abroad) if they deal with the letting themselves; however, they will apply to all properties let through letting agents if the agent's standard form of

A landlord says ...

'Do not let a tenant in until the paperwork is signed.'

tenancy agreement is used. They will not apply however to lettings to another business, for example company lets.

The regulations do not cover what are called 'core terms'. These are terms setting the price (i.e. the rent) and terms defining the subject matter of the contract (i.e. describing the property to be let). They may, however, apply to rent review clauses. A standard term is unfair if it creates a significant imbalance in the parties' rights and obligations under the contract, to the detriment of the consumer, and contrary to the requirement of good faith. The regulations are aimed at terms which have the effect of reducing the consumers' rights under the ordinary rules of contract or the general law. The regulations also require that plain and intelligible language is used and a term is open to challenge if it is difficult to understand by the ordinary person. The requirement of plain language applies to all terms, including core terms.

The fact that one term in an agreement has been found unfair does not affect the validity of the rest of the agreement. It is just that clause which will be unenforceable.

In the context of tenancy agreements, the types of clauses that have come under consideration so far are unintelligible and unfair rent review clauses, misleading forfeiture clauses, and penalty clauses. These are all discussed below.

Consumers (or tenants) who have a complaint about a contract term can refer it to their local trading standards office who may in turn refer it to the Unfair Contract Terms Unit at the Office of Fair Trading (whose address is in Appendix 1). However, the main effect of an unfair term is that it is void and will not be enforced by a court in legal proceedings. So if rent is increased by a rent review term which is found to be unfair, a landlord will not be able to obtain a county court judgment in respect of the unpaid excess rent or obtain a possession order on the grounds of those rent arrears. He will also probably face an order to pay the tenant's legal costs.

Individual terms you will need in the agreement ━━━━━━━━━

Essential terms

Details of the following information **must** be provided by the landlord to the tenant whether there is a written tenancy agreement or not. It is a criminal offence for a landlord to fail to provide this information to a tenant within 28 days of a request (unless he has a reasonable excuse, such as being on holiday).

The tenancy's commencement date

It is important that the tenancy is dated and that it is clear from the document, the date on which the tenancy started. As set out in chapter 1, the law governing a tenancy depends upon when the tenancy was initially granted. There may be new laws in the future which affect tenants' rights. If the tenancy goes on a long time, it may become difficult to prove exactly when the tenancy started if this is not set out in the agreement. For this reason you should always keep a copy of the first tenancy agreement, even if subsequent agreements are given to the tenant. As regards the subsequent agreements, they should of course also be kept. You will need to know the precise date the current or last fixed term started, for working out when the fixed term ends, and the days in the month or week when subsequent periodic tenancies begin and end. This information is necessary if you have to serve any Section 21 Notices (notices requiring possession – see chapter 8).

The commencement date of a tenancy is also important for working out what day in the week or month the rent runs from. Normally rent is payable on the day of the month or week which is the anniversary of the commencement date, e.g. if the tenancy started on Monday 3rd January, a monthly rent will fall due on the 3rd day of every subsequent month and weekly rent will fall due every Monday. Landlords who let several properties usually like all rent to be paid on the same day, usually the 1st of the month, and if so, the agreement should stipulate that rent is payable on that day. To prevent confusion, it might be wise in this case for the agreement to provide for the tenant to pay an irregular amount for the first month (calculated on a daily basis) so that the rent will run from the stipulated payment day, if the tenancy actually commenced on another day. So if the tenancy starts on 20th January, the tenant will pay 12 days' rent up to 31st January and then the full month's rent on the 1st day of every month thereafter.

The term

It is normal practice for a tenancy agreement to be for a fixed term, and the most common fixed term is six months. The legal effect of a fixed term is that you cannot evict the tenant (other than under the 'bad tenant' grounds – see chapter 8) and the tenant is liable for the rent, for its duration. So if in a six-month term the tenant moves out after four months, you can still claim the remaining two months rent from him. The exception to this is if you re-let the property to someone else after he has gone, as you cannot claim rent twice. Of course, you can always end the fixed term by agreement with the tenant – the point is that you do not have to. However, in practice you should always try to 'mitigate your losses' by re-letting to another tenant if this is possible.

It is wise when letting to new tenants not to make the term too long. Tenants are not always as satisfactory as they seem when you initially interview them. For example they may continually pay late, causing administration problems, or you may receive complaints about their behaviour from neighbours. If you have a six-month AST you can simply serve a notice requiring possession on them to expire at the end of the six month period and then if they fail to move out you can evict them (see chapter 8). The tenants may object to this but there is nothing they can do about it. However, if you have given them a 12-month tenancy, you will have to wait until the end of the 12 months to get them out. If the tenants prove satisfactory, they can always stay on at the property at the end of the term, either under a new fixed term agreement or under a periodic tenancy.

Another reason for going for a six-month tenancy is that yearly tenancies will attract a higher stamp duty (if this is payable). Also, in an AST the tenant has the right to refer the rent to the Rent Assessment Committee during the first six months. If the Committee decide to fix a new rent, this will apply to the whole of the fixed term, even if there is a rent review clause in the agreement.

The rent

It is important that there is no dispute over the rent and the amount should clearly be stated in the agreement, together with the period of payment. It is generally best to make this monthly, as most people get paid monthly now. However, for some HMO properties you may feel it best to collect rent weekly on the basis that the tenants are likely to be more able and willing to pay smaller weekly sums that larger monthly ones. You should in all agreements specify that the rent is payable in advance, otherwise the law will imply that it is payable in arrears. You can also set out in the agreement the method the rent is to be paid, for example by standing order into a specified bank account. The agreement should state that the rent is payable without 'deduction or set-off'. For a discussion about the date rent is to be paid see the paragraph on the commencement date above.

If rent is to be paid weekly, the landlord is required by law to provide the tenant with a rent book, available from legal stationers.

Other important terms

The following are other important terms, most of which should always be included in the agreement. However, unlike the terms above, you will not be potentially liable under the criminal law if they are omitted.

A description of the property

This sounds obvious, but you should be careful to define the property accurately. If the tenancy agreement is for a room in a shared house for example, make sure that all the rooms have names or numbers (and do not change them). Flats should be clearly described: first floor or ground floor etc. – again it is a good idea to number them. You should also make it clear if any part of the property is excluded. For example, in a large property with outbuildings, some of these might be separately let as garages to neighbours or used to store your own property. The agreement should make it clear which of these are part of the letting and which are excluded.

Payments other than rent

The agreement should make it quite clear which payments will be made by the tenant and which by the landlord. For example:

- **Council Tax** – this will usually be payable by the tenant, but for HMOs it is normally payable by the landlord.

- **Water charges** – if there is no express provision, then they will be the tenant's responsibility. However, often the landlord will accept responsibility. Landlords should be wary of this though if the supply is metered.

- **Utilities** – for ASTs and ATs, these are almost invariably paid by the tenant. However, in house-sharing arrangements, they may be paid by the landlord, particularly if he is a resident landlord.

Tip

If utilities are to be in the tenant's name, it is best to arrange this before he moves in.

For all payments where the landlord is responsible, the agreement should provide for the rent to be increased if the payments are increased, so the landlord is not out of pocket.

Penalty clauses

Tenancy agreements (particularly those drafted by some letting agents) sometimes include stringent penalty clauses, for example for late payment of rent. However, these are now liable to be found void under the Unfair Terms Regulations and a landlord needs to be careful when using them. The following are examples of clauses that are often used:

- A clause providing for interest on late payment of rent. This is a standard clause. Unless the rate of interest is excessive, this will not fall foul of the regulations. Indeed, this type of clause is recommended, otherwise a landlord will only be able to claim interest on unpaid rent if he brings court proceedings. A typical clause of this type will provide for interest to be paid at three or four per cent above the bank base rate.

- A clause providing for a fixed penalty for non-payment of rent. If this is used instead of an interest clause and is for a modest sum, then it will probably be found to be fair, if challenged. A landlord could justifiably say that it was to make the agreement clearer and to get rid of complicated interest calculations. However, if it is in addition to an interest clause and/or is for a punitive amount, e.g. £5 per day, it may not be upheld.

- Clauses providing for fixed fees for administration expenses; for example, stating that charges of £X will be charged per occasion when rent is paid other than in the manner specified in the agreement (e.g. not by standing order); stating that £X will be charged every time the property is visited to collect or pursue late rent or every time a letter is sent demanding unpaid rent; stating that £X will be charged every time an appointment is missed. If these clauses reflect a genuine expense that the landlord will incur, then they may be reasonable. However, if they are in the nature of a penalty they are vulnerable to challenge. For example a 'missed appointments' clause would be fair if it was charged in respect of missed appointments made at the tenant's request and if the sum charged genuinely reflected the landlord's expenses.

Note

Any unusual clauses in the agreement should be given prominence, e.g. by having them in bold type.

If it is important to the landlord that a clause of this nature (other than a standard clause for interest) is included in the tenancy agreement, it would be wise to specifically draw it to the attention of the tenant at the time he signs the agreement and explain it to him. If he agrees to it, you should ask him to initial the clause in the agreement. This would give the landlord some protection if the tenant subsequently challenges the clause.

The deposit

You should always take a deposit from tenants and the agreement should specify the amount of the deposit and how it is to be used. There are probably more disputes about damage deposits than anything else; landlords complain that tenants leave owing rent equal to or more than the value of the deposit so they are out of pocket if there are repairs needed, and tenants complain that landlords routinely retain deposits without good cause. It is usually very important to tenants that deposits are returned, as they need the money to pay the deposit for their next rented property.

Your agreement should therefore be very clear about deposits and should deal with the following points:

- The amount of the deposit. It is usual for this to be the equivalent of one month's rent. It should not be for more than two months' rent, otherwise it will be held to be a premium, which is inadvisable.

- What the landlord can use the deposit for – e.g. damage to the premises or furniture, unpaid rent and services, and also any sum repayable to the local authority when Housing Benefit has been paid direct to the landlord.

- A requirement that a tenant should make up the deposit if the landlord has to use part of it during the tenancy, e.g. for repairs.

- Whether the tenant shall be entitled to interest on the deposit (normally the agreement provides that interest will not be paid).

- When the deposit is to be returned to the tenant – normally this is when the tenant gives up possession of the property, however it is a good idea for the agreement to provide that if the tenant's Housing Benefit has been paid direct to the landlord, the landlord is entitled to hold the deposit until he is sure that there will be no claw-back. He can, however, only retain the deposit for a reasonable period of time.

- The agreement should also state that the tenant is not entitled to withhold rent on the grounds that the landlord is holding a deposit. However be warned that this will not always stop a tenant from leaving without paying his last month's rent!

There are often misunderstandings about the way deposits should be dealt with, particularly when proceedings are being brought for possession on the basis of rent arrears. While the tenant is in the property, the deposit is held by the landlord as security and should not be credited to the tenant against unpaid rent. When the tenant leaves, the landlord will inspect the property, and assess its condition. The damage deposit should then be used as follows:

1. If there are any repairs that need to be done or items to be replaced, the cost of this will be deducted from the deposit. It may also be necessary to clean the property and again the costs of this will normally be deducted. It should be emphasised that costs must be reasonable and landlords should keep all receipts. There may be other deductions that are appropriate (e.g. if there has been a local authority claw-back). However, all deductions from the deposit must be authorised by the relevant clause in the tenancy agreement.

2. After these costs have been deducted, and only after this, the remaining money is credited to any rent arrears due.

3. The balance (if any) is then paid to the tenant.

Ideally, the landlord will inspect the property with the tenant (who will not be in arrears) the day the tenant leaves, the property will be in perfect condition, and the landlord will hand the deposit back there and then. If there are deductions that need to be made, you should deal with any work quickly so as not to delay returning any remaining balance to the tenant.

Because of the perceived problem with damage deposits, the government is considering introducing statutory regulation. The National Federation of Residential Landlords has been lobbying to prevent this, and to ensure that a voluntary scheme is introduced that will allow landlords to retain possession of the damage deposit. At the time of writing, a non-custodial tenancy deposit scheme is being launched in five pilot areas in England and Wales. Under this scheme, participating landlords will be bonded (i.e. covered by insurance) and there is a cheap and quick arbitration scheme in the event of any dispute. Further informa-

Tip

Make sure, if you are using a letting agent, that he has a client's money protection scheme as damage deposits held by him will be at risk if he goes out of business.

tion can be obtained from your local landlords association or from the Independent Housing Ombudsman (whose address is in Appendix 1).

Rent review

As set out in chapter 7, you can normally only increase the rent either by agreement (usually by the tenant signing a new tenancy agreement at an increased rent), or by serving a notice of increase. A tenant may refuse to sign a new tenancy agreement and new rents in notices of increase can be referred to the Rent Assessment Committee. Rent usually cannot be increased at all during the fixed term. These potential problems can be overcome by including a clause providing for rent review in the tenancy agreement. It is important that this clause is as clear as possible and that any mechanism for calculating any new rent is easily understood and fair, to prevent the clause falling foul of the unfair terms in consumer contracts regulations.

There are different types of rent review clauses. Some of them provide a mechanism for rent to be increased at specified periods by way of reference to a government index such as the retail price index. Others simply provide for the landlord to increase the rent at specified periods, but allow the tenant to give notice to terminate the agreement if he does not agree to it.

Most tenancy agreements nowadays, however, do not include rent review clauses because if a tenancy is a short (e.g. six month) AST, the landlord can simply serve a section 21 notice and evict the tenant if he refuses to sign a new agreement at a higher rent.

Repairs and redecoration

Most landlords have statutory repairing obligations which they cannot contract out of (see chapters 4 and 7), but the agreement should state who is responsible for non-structural repairs and re-decoration, which are not covered by statute. However, you will not wish your tenant to re-decorate the property by painting all the walls black, so it is usual to include a clause either prohibiting them from doing any re-decoration at all without the landlord's written permission or from re-decorating in anything other than the existing style and colours. If the property includes a garden, the agreement should include a clause requiring the tenant to maintain it. Alternatively you may wish the agreement to provide for access for your gardener (his charges to be included in the rent).

Damage and alterations

The law prohibits tenants from deliberately damaging the property, and it is normal for this to be specifically set out in the agreement. Usually there are separate clauses relating to the property and its furniture. The law, however, does not prohibit 'improvements' and therefore the agreement should specifically prohibit any alterations to the property. It is also a good idea to include a separate clause prohibiting the tenant from changing the locks and authorising you to retain a set of keys (for access in the case of emergency).

Use

As the law allows a tenant to use the property for whatever purpose he wants, it is advisable to include a clause restricting use of the property to that of a single, private, residential dwelling, and to include clauses forbidding anti-social behaviour (i.e. causing a nuisance to other tenants and neighbours).

Access

The agreement should specify that the landlord (or his agent) should be permitted to enter and inspect the property upon giving reasonable notice in writing (say 48 hours) to the tenant, but it should also state that in cases of real emergency this requirement will not apply. This is important, as you will need access to carry out regular inspections, do any repairs, and to have the annual gas safety checks done.

Assignment and sub-letting

Assignment is where ownership of the tenancy agreement as a whole is transferred from one person to another; sub-letting is where part or all of the property is let under a separate agreement.

It is essential that there are express covenants against assignment and sub-letting, as there is little point in carefully vetting your

A landlord says ...

'The worst thing about being a landlord is tenants ringing in the middle of the night because they have lost their keys.'

tenants if they can then assign or sub-let to whoever they wish. It should be clear from the agreement that the prohibition is absolute.

Insurance

The landlord will usually arrange for insurance cover, and the agreement should prohibit the tenant from activity which will affect the validity of the insurance cover and also provide for him to be responsible for any increase in the insurance premiums due to his behaviour. The tenant will usually be responsible for the insurance of his own belongings. For more details about insurance see chapter 4.

Tenants' property left behind

Tenants often go, leaving items at the property which can cause problems for the landlord. If the landlord throws away property which subsequently turns out to be of value, he may be subject to a claim from the tenant for damages. It is wise therefore to include a term in the agreement allowing the landlord to dispose of any items left at the property.

Address for service

Under section 48 of the Landlord and Tenant Act 1987, no rent is lawfully due from a tenant unless and until the landlord has given the tenant notice in writing of an address in England and Wales at which notices (including notices in proceedings) can be served on him. It is best that this notice is included in the tenancy agreement. The address can be the address of the landlord's agent. This clause is particularly important for landlords who are resident abroad.

It is also a good idea to specify that any notices or other documents shall be deemed properly served on the tenant by either being left at the premises or by being sent there by first-class post.

Forfeiture

This is an essential clause, as it allows you to evict the tenant during the fixed term under certain circumstances (e.g. as specified in the Housing Act 1988). The actual wording of most standard forfeiture clauses is somewhat misleading as it states that in certain specified circumstances (i.e. if rent is unpaid for 14 days) the landlord can re-enter and the tenancy will be 'determined' (ended). Of course the landlord cannot physically re-enter the property himself: physical re-entry can only be done by a court bailiff pursuant to a possession order. This should be made clear as otherwise the clause may fall foul of the Unfair Terms Regulations. However, you should be careful about altering the wording of a forfeiture clause unless you know what you are doing, as you may alter its effect. A suitable form of wording would be:

> If the Tenant fails to pay the rent (or any part) within 14 days of the due date or fails to comply with his obligations under this Agreement or if any of the circumstances mentioned in Grounds 2 or 8 of Part 1 of Schedule 2 or Grounds 10–15 of Part II of Schedule 2 of the Housing Act 1988 arise the Landlord may re-enter the Property and end the tenancy. This right of re-entry is not to be exercised by the Landlord without a court order while anyone is residing in the Property or while the tenancy is an assured tenancy. The Landlord retains all his other rights in respect of the Tenants' obligations under this Agreement.

If the tenancy agreement you are using does not state that the right of re-entry can only be pursuant to a court order, the penultimate sentence in the clause above should be added as this makes it clear that the 're-entry' can only be after a court order has been obtained. This prevents the clause from being misleading.

Other prohibitions, etc

There is a number of things landlords may not want the tenant to do, which can be set out in the agreement, for example:

- Keeping pets/animals at the property.

- Using any heating other than specified heating provided and in particular not to use oil heaters.

- Leaving the property vacant for more than 30 days.

Remember that you have no control over the tenant once he is in the property. The only way you can legally influence how he treats the property is through the tenancy agreement.

Non-shorthold tenancies

Your own home

If you are letting your own home, you may wish to consider letting the property on an AT rather than an AST. This is because landlords letting their own home have an additional mandatory ground for possession, and therefore do not need to rely on the shorthold ground. If it is decided to do this, it is essential that the agreement contains a notice to this effect. A suitable form of notice could be:

> 'The Landlord hereby notifies the Tenant that possession of the Premises may be recovered under Ground 1 of Schedule 2 to the Housing Act 1988 (under which the Court must order possession of the Premises where the Landlord has previously occupied the Premises as his only or principal home or requires the Premises as the only or principal home for the Landlord or the Landlord's spouse).'

Provided (and **only** if) the above clause is inserted, you should then insert a clause specifying that the agreement is not an assured shorthold tenancy, e.g.

> 'It is not intended that this agreement will create an assured shorthold tenancy.'

You should be very careful about taking away the shorthold status of the tenancy if you have not yet lived in the property as your main home (for example if you intend it to be your retirement home), as if you later decide not to live in the property, you may not be able to recover possession at all. In these circumstances it is probably best to keep the tenancy as a shorthold one.

This section is in respect of property where the landlord has moved out. Where the landlord continues to live at the property, see the section on resident landlords in chapter 1.

Out-of-season holiday accommodation

There are other circumstances where a mandatory ground for possession is available and where a landlord may wish to consider removing the shorthold status of the tenancy. The only one which is appropriate to consider in the context of the private landlord is out-of-season lets of holiday properties. This is where a property which is let out as a holiday home for part of the year, e.g. in the summer, is let as an ordinary residential letting during the winter months. For this ground to be available, the property must have been occupied for holiday purposes at some time during the 12 months prior to the granting of the tenancy and the letting must be for a fixed term of not more than eight months. The letting must be for a fixed term, not a periodic term, which means that a formal tenancy agreement is essential. The agreement should include a term removing the shorthold status, as set out above, and a notice informing the tenant that this ground will apply must be served at the commencement of the tenancy.

Inventory

If the property is let furnished, you should prepare a detailed inventory of the contents which should be attached to the agreement. The inventory should also give details about items, for example whether they are new or damaged, and perhaps with electrical items the date when they were last checked. This will help prevent arguments later about their condition. Separate columns might be useful for items to be ticked at the end (and perhaps the start) of the tenancy. The inventory should ideally be signed by both landlord and tenant. It is a good idea to include a term in the agreement stating that the condition of the premises and its contents will be deemed to be in good order unless the tenant notifies the landlord to the contrary within a specified time period (say five days).

There are professional companies that can provide an inventory service, and you may find this helpful, particularly for a first let or if you have a number of properties. You should look for a firm which is a member of the Association of Independent Inventory Clerks. Your landlords' association should be able to advise you of any local firms.

Guarantees

If you intend to have a guarantor, he can either sign the tenancy agreement itself, in which case it should contain a paragraph specifying the circumstances under which he will become liable, or he can sign a separate form of guarantee. Remember that a guarantor will only be liable for terms that are brought to his attention at the time he signs the guarantee and not for any subsequent terms that may be agreed with the tenant. The guarantor should therefore sign a fresh form of guarantee every time a new agreement is signed by the tenant.

Stamp Duty

This is a government tax payable on tenancy agreements, which is recorded by a stamp on the document. It was previously only 50p in many cases and was often left unpaid. This is inadvisable, as although an unstamped tenancy agreement is still valid, it cannot be used in evidence in court proceedings. In the past judges have often turned a blind eye to the fact that an agreement is unstamped. But there is no guarantee that this will continue.

At the time of writing, the threshold for stamp duty has been increased to an annual rent of £5,000 which means that many agreements will now no longer need to be stamped. If the rent is more than this, you should check with the Stamp Office the amount of duty payable. The amount of stamp duty will depend upon the length of the term, the average annual rent, and the amount of any premium. Duty is not generally payable for agreements for furnished properties with a fixed term of less than one year, unless the annual rent exceeds £5,000, in which there will be a fixed duty of £5. Both need to be stamped. If a document is not stamped within 30 days, there will be a penalty payable.

The landlord can specify in the agreement that the cost of stamp duty should be borne by the tenant, and it would be wise for him to arrange for the documents to be stamped himself. This is done by sending the documents and a cheque to the nearest Inland Revenue Stamp Office.

Obtaining tenancy agreements

Law Pack produce excellent forms of tenancy agreement for use in a variety of circumstances: see example of **Law Pack**'s Furnished House and Flat Rental Agreement on the next pages. Also, see panel advertisement at back of guide for details or visit www.lawpack.co.uk. Landlord associations will often provide forms of tenancy agreement for their members, or forms can be purchased from legal stationers. If, however, you feel that any special terms are needed for your property, it is best to get a tenancy agreement drafted by a solicitor. Be sure to choose a solicitor who specialises in residential landlord and tenant work.

Tip

Further information about Stamp Duty can be obtained from the Inland Revenue helpline (see Appendix 1).

Tip

You may also consider giving new tenants an information pack about the property. For example, this could contain details about appliances and how to operate them, where the fuse box, gas and electricity meters are, information about fire safety, and the landlord's telephone number to ring in the case of emergency. For holiday properties landlords could also give details of local amenities.

Completed example of Law Pack assured shorthold tenancy agreement

F201

TENANCY AGREEMENT
(For a Furnished House or Flat on an Assured Shorthold Tenancy)

The **PROPERTY** *Flat B, 14 Gladstone Street, Ashbourne, Derbyshire DE2 4AX*

The **LANDLORD** *RON ROBERTS of 7 Percy Street, Ashbourne, Derbyshire DE2 5A2* and

of *TIM BOND of 7 Bath Road, Bristol BS2 3DJ*

The **TENANT** *STEVE ROBERTS, JOHN STEEL, AMANDA JAMES* and

SUSAN SHAW

(*delete as appropriate)

The **TERM** *NINE* months beginning on *13th August 2000* of each week/month* payable in advance on the *13th* of each ~~week~~/month*

The **RENT** £ *500* per week/~~month~~* payable in advance

The **DEPOSIT** £ *500*

The **INVENTORY** means the list of the Landlord's possessions at the Property which has been signed by the Landlord and the Tenant

DATED *13th August 2000*

SIGNED

Ron Roberts
T. Bond

(The Landlord)

S. Roberts
J. Steel
Amanda James
Susan Shaw

(The Tenant)

THIS TENANCY AGREEMENT comprises the particulars detailed above and the terms and conditions printed overleaf whereby the Property is hereby let by the Landlord and taken by the Tenant for the Term at the Rent.

IMPORTANT NOTICE TO LANDLORDS:
(1) The details of 'The LANDLORD' near the top of this Agreement must include an address for the Landlord in England or Wales as well as his/her name.
(2) Always remember to give the written Notice to Terminate to the Tenant two clear months before the end of the Term.

IMPORTANT NOTICE TO TENANTS:
(1) In general, if you currently occupy this Property under a protected or statutory tenancy and you give it up to take a new tenancy of the same or other accommodation owned by the same Landlord, that tenancy cannot be an Assured Shorthold Tenancy and this Agreement is not appropriate.
(2) If you currently occupy this Property under an Assured Tenancy which is not an Assured Shorthold Tenancy your Landlord is not permitted to grant you an Assured Shorthold Tenancy of this Property or of alternative property.

(Continued on next page)

64

Completed example of Law Pack assured shorthold tenancy agreement *(continued)*

Terms and Conditions

1. This Agreement is intended to create an assured shorthold tenancy as defined in the Housing Act 1988, as amended by the Housing Act 1996, and the provisions for the recovery of possession by the Landlord in that Act apply accordingly. The Tenant understands that the Landlord will be entitled to recover possession of the Property at the end of the Term.

2. The Tenant will:

 2.1 pay the Rent at the times and in the manner aforesaid without any deduction abatement or set-off whatsoever (save for any deduction abatement or set-off allowable in law)

 2.2 pay all charges in respect of any electric, gas, water and telephonic or televisual services used at or supplied to the Property and Council Tax or any similar tax that might be charged in addition to or replacement of it during the Term

 2.3 keep the items on the Inventory and the interior of the Property in a good and clean state and condition and not damage or injure the Property or the items on the Inventory

 2.4 yield up the Property and the items on the Inventory at the end of the Term in the same clean state and condition it/they was/were in at the beginning of the Term (but the Tenant will not be responsible for fair wear and tear caused during normal use of the Property and the items on the Inventory or for any damage covered by and recoverable under the insurance policy effected by the Landlord under clause 3.2)

 2.5 not make any alteration or addition to the Property nor without the Landlord's prior written consent do any redecoration or painting of the Property

 2.6 not do anything on or at the Property which:

 (a) may be or become a nuisance or annoyance to the Landlord or owners or occupiers of adjoining or nearby premises

 (b) is illegal or immoral

 (c) may in any way affect the validity of the insurance of the Property and the items listed on the Inventory or cause an increase in the premium payable by the Landlord

 2.7 not without the Landlord's prior consent allow or keep any pet or any kind of animal at the Property

 2.8 not use or occupy the Property in any way whatsoever other than as a private residence

 2.9 not assign, sublet, charge or part with or share possession or occupation of the Property

 2.10 permit the Landlord or anyone authorised by the Landlord at reasonable hours in the daytime and upon reasonable prior notice (except in emergency) to enter and view the Property and the items on the Inventory for any proper purpose (including the checking of compliance with the Tenant's obligations under this Agreement and during the last month of the Term the showing of the Property to prospective new tenants)

 2.11 pay interest at the rate of 4% above the Base Lending Rate for the time being of the Landlord's bankers upon any Rent or other money due from the Tenant under this Agreement which is more than 3 days in arrear in respect of the period from when it became due to the date of payment

3. The Landlord will:

 3.1 for as long as the Tenant performs his obligations under this Agreement allow the Tenant peaceably to hold and enjoy the Property during the term without lawful interruption from the Landlord or any person rightfully claiming under or in trust for the Landlord

 3.2 insure the Property and the items listed on the Inventory and use all reasonable efforts to arrange for any damage caused by an insured risk to be remedied as soon as possible

 3.3 keep in repair the structure and exterior of the Property (including drains gutters and external pipes)

 keep in repair and proper working order the installations at the Property for the supply of water, gas and electricity and for sanitation (including basins, sinks, baths and sanitary conveniences)

 keep in repair and proper working order the installation at the Property for space heating and heating water

 But the Landlord will not be required to:

 carry out works for which the Tenant is responsible by virtue of his/her duty to use the Property in a tenant-like manner

 reinstate the Property in the case of damage or destruction if the insurers refuse to pay out the insurance money due to anything the Tenant has done or failed to do

 rebuild or reinstate the Property in the case of destruction or damage of the Property by a risk not covered by the policy of insurance effected by the Landlord

4. If at any time

 4.1 any part of the Rent is outstanding for 10 days after becoming due (whether formally demanded or not) and/or

 4.2 there is any breach, non-observance or non-performance by the Tenant of any covenant or other term of this Agreement which has been notified in writing to the Tenant and the Tenant has failed within a reasonable period of time to remedy the breach and/or pay reasonable compensation to the Landlord for the breach and/or

 4.3 any interim receiver is appointed in respect of the Tenant's property or Bankruptcy Orders made in respect of the Tenant or the Tenant makes any arrangement with his creditors or suffers any distress or execution to be levied on his goods and/or

 4.4 any of the grounds set out as Grounds 8 or Grounds 10-15 (inclusive) (which relate to breach of any obligation by a Tenant) contained in the Housing Act 1988 Schedule 2 apply

 the Landlord may enter the Property (and upon such re-entry this Agreement shall absolutely determine but without prejudice to any claim which the Landlord may have against the Tenant in respect of any antecedent breach of any covenant or any term of this Agreement). This right of re-entry is not to be exercised by the Landlord without a court order while anyone is residing in the Property or while the tenancy is an assured tenancy

5. 5.1 The Deposit will be held by the Landlord in an interest bearing bank or building society account and will be refunded to the Tenant at the end of the Term (however it ends) but less any deductions properly made by the Landlord to cover any breaches of the obligations in his Agreement by the Tenant

 5.2 If at any time during the Term the Landlord is obliged to deduct from the Deposit to satisfy any breaches of the obligations of the Tenant the Tenant shall make such additional payments as are necessary to restore the full amount of the Deposit

6. The Landlord hereby notifies the Tenant under Section 48 of the Landlord & Tenant Act 1987 that any notices (including notices in proceedings) should be served upon the Landlord at the address stated with the name of the Landlord overleaf

7. Any notices or other documents shall be deemed served on the Tenant by either being left at the Property or by being sent to the Tenant at the Property by first-class post. If notices or other documents are served on the Tenant by post they shall be deemed served on the day after posting

8. Any person other than the Tenant who pays the rent due hereunder or any part thereof to the Landlord shall be deemed to have made such payment as agent for and on behalf of the Tenant which the Landlord shall be entitled to assume without enquiry

9. Should any article, rubbish, or vehicle remain on or within the Property for more than 7 days after the determination of the tenancy it is hereby agreed that the Landlord shall dispose of the same in such manner as he thinks fit at the Tenant's expense and that any proceeds of sale be placed in a trust account for the Tenant

10. In the event of damage to or destruction of the Property by any of the risks insured against by the Landlord the Tenant shall be relieved from payment of the Rent to the extent that the Tenant's use and enjoyment of the Property is thereby prevented and from performance of its obligations as to the state and condition of the Property to the extent of and so long as there prevails such damage or destruction (except to the extent that the insurance is prejudiced by any act or default of the Tenant) the amount in case of dispute to be settled by arbitration

11. Where the context so admits:

 8.1 The 'Landlord' includes the persons from time to time entitled to receive the Rent

 8.2 The 'Tenant' includes any persons deriving title under the Tenant

 8.3 The 'Property' includes any part or parts of the Property and all of the Landlord's fixtures and fittings at or upon the Property

 8.4 The 'Term' shall mean the period stated in the particulars overleaf or any shorter or longer period in the event of an earlier termination or an extension or holding over respectively

12. All references to the singular shall include the plural and vice versa and any obligations or liabilities of more than one person shall be joint and several and an obligation on the part of a party shall include an obligation not to allow or permit the breach of that obligation

8201040

During the tenancy

6

The covenant of quiet enjoyment ──────

Every tenancy agreement contains what is called the 'covenant of quiet enjoyment'. This does not mean just that tenants are entitled to a noise-free environment, but that they have the right to live in the property undisturbed. This means not only that they have the right not to be illegally evicted, but also that the landlord should respect their rights and not do anything that will adversely affect their occupation of the property.

The covenant of quiet enjoyment is most commonly invoked to protect tenants whose landlord is trying to 'persuade' them to leave, perhaps because they are not paying the rent or because he wants the property back for his own uses, but is reluctant to go to court for a possession order. For example, such landlords may constantly visit the property, shout threats at the tenant, and interrupt the gas and electricity supply. This sort of behaviour is illegal and can attract both a criminal charge and make the landlord liable for civil proceedings for an injunction and/or damages. However, the covenant for quiet enjoyment can also apply to other matters, for example it can cover a landlord's failure to comply with his repairing covenants.

It is important therefore that landlords ensure that they are complying with all their covenants, including their obligations to keep the property in proper repair (see below), and that they do not intrude on the tenant's privacy. These may conflict, as clearly the landlord will have to go to the property from time to time to carry out his inspections and repairing obligations. Some tenants may object to this and call it harassment (particularly if they are in arrears of rent). If there is a problem of this nature or is likely to be, then the landlord should take care to only attend at the property by appointment or by the invitation of the tenant. He should never use his keys to enter the property without the tenants' knowledge or permission, other than in cases of genuine emergency.

A landlord who treats his tenants with respect and who complies with his obligations under the tenancy will also be protecting himself from any potential claims from his tenants. He will also find it easier to enforce his own rights against the tenants, should this be necessary.

Although a covenant of quiet enjoyment is not implied into licence agreements, licensees have the right to use the property for the purpose for which occupation was granted, which gives them a certain amount of similar protection for the duration of the licence agreement.

Rent matters ——————————————————

The rent book

If the rent is payable weekly, then a landlord has a legal obligation to provide a tenant with a rent book. This must contain certain prescribed information but rent books can easily be bought at law stationers. **Law Pack** also produce a form of rent book. There is no legal requirement to provide a rent book if rent is paid monthly.

Collecting rent

In most tenancies the rent will be paid by the tenants by standing order. However many HMO tenants do not have bank accounts and will pay cash. For these types of tenants, often the only way the landlord can ensure that he gets paid is to go round and collect the rent personally. Collecting rent is a also good opportunity to inspect the property.

Good times to collect rent are either on Friday afternoons or Sunday mornings. Many people get paid on Friday so this is a good time to catch a tenant before he has had an opportunity to spend it. If a tenant is trying to avoid you, Sunday morning is the most inconvenient time for him to disappear.

Be careful, however, when collecting rent, that you do not lay yourself open to a charge of harassment. Be polite at all times, and never enter the property unless you are invited to do so by the tenant. If a tenant is in arrears, do not call round more frequently than normal (unless at the tenant's request). If the tenant makes a formal complaint about you, stop calling round altogether and make all future demands for rent in writing. You will also at this stage probably want to consider whether to start eviction proceedings – see chapter 7. If you think that the tenant is at all likely to make a claim against you for harassment, it is a good idea to keep a diary describing all contact with the tenant, giving dates and details of conversations.

Increasing the rent

If a tenant stays in a property for many years, the landlord will need to increase the rent from time to time. This can be done in one of the following ways:

For assured and assured shorthold tenancies:

- By agreement with the tenant. This is usually done by granting the tenant a new fixed term agreement at a new rent. If rent is increased by agreement it cannot be subsequently challenged by the tenant.

- Pursuant to a rent review clause in the tenancy agreement. Again, if the terms of the rent review clause are followed properly, it is unlikely that the tenant will be able to challenge the new rent as he will be deemed to have agreed to this by signing the tenancy agreement in the first place (subject to the clause not being in breach of the Unfair Contract Terms Regulations).

- By serving a notice of increase. This is has to be in the prescribed form, which can be purchased from law stationers. The new rent should take effect from the beginning of a new period of the tenancy, or after a minimum period of one month for a weekly tenancy. It cannot take effect during a fixed term, only during a periodic tenancy i.e. after the fixed term has expired. A landlord can only increase the rent by notice once a year. If a tenant is unhappy with the new proposed rent he can refer it to the Rent Assessment Committee (see below).

For Rent Act tenancies:

Although this book has been written more for new landlords rather than Rent Act landlords (i.e. landlords of properties where tenancies pre-date 15th January 1989), it is useful to consider Rent Act tenancies in this context. A Rent Act tenant has a right to apply to the Rent Officer to fix a 'fair rent' which is then registered and is the maximum rent the landlord is allowed to charge the tenant. The landlord can apply to have the fair rent re-registered every two years, or before this if the circumstances of the letting or the condition of the property have changed. Thus, if the property is substantially improved by the landlord, he can then apply to have the rent increased within the two-year period. Both parties can challenge the rent assessed by the Rent Officer by referring it to the local Rent Assessment Committee.

Prior to 1989, fair rents were notoriously low and this was a disincentive for people to let property. Since the Housing Act 1988, landlords have been able to let properties at a market rent and this, together with the right to recover property under the short-hold ground, has meant that there are far more rented properties around. This in turn is having an effect on fair rents for Rent Act tenancies, as Rent Officers are now having to take these market rents into account when fixing the fair rent. As a result of this, Rent Act fair rents are tending to increase, in some areas substantially. If you are the owner of a property which has Rent Act tenants, you should bear this in mind when applying to have the fair rent increased – it might even be worthwhile taking some professional advice on the level of rent which is now achievable. Bear in mind that although the market rent is now the starting point for Rent Officers in determining fair rents, they will then make deductions: for example, if the tenant has carried out improvements, or if the property is in poor condition, or was originally let unfurnished.

Note

The Rent Office holds a register of fair rents which is open to inspection by the public.

Challenges to the rent - the Rent Assessment Committee

In certain circumstances an assured tenant can challenge the rent and ask the Rent Assessment Committee to review it:

- For assured shorthold tenancies only, during the first six months of the tenancy.

- After a notice of increase of rent (see above) has been served on the tenant.

Unlike Rent Act tenancies, the tenant cannot refer the rent to the Rent Officer and his only role with assured and assured shorthold tenancies is assessing rents for the purpose of Housing Benefit payments.

When a rent is referred to the Rent Assessment Committee, they will then notify the other party and both parties will be asked to make written representations. The rent can be either considered on the written representations alone or either party can request a hearing.

The application will be considered by a panel drawn from the committee's members. Panel members can either be lawyers, valuers, or lay members. There is always a valuer on every committee, and the valuer will be one who has good local knowledge of the area where the property is situated. For a hearing, the panel will normally consist of three members; for considering written representations, it may be only two.

Even if there is going to be a hearing, written representations and evidence should be sent to the panel **at least seven days** before the hearing. This is because the rules require copies to be served on the other side so they can be given a reasonable opportunity to consider it. If evidence is provided too close to the hearing date you will risk having the hearing adjourned, particularly if the tenant does not attend the hearing.

What the panel has to consider is (in the case of ASTs only):

1. Is there a sufficient number of dwellings let on assured tenancies in the area for the panel to be able to do a comparison? If yes, then:

2.   Is the rent significantly higher than the level of rents in the locality (i.e. more than about 5–10%)? If yes, then:

3.   What is the market rent for this tenancy? And,

4.   From what date should any new rent start?

For ATs (not shortholds), the panel only has to consider questions 3 and 4.

The following points may assist you if you have had a property referred to the Rent Assessment Committee:

- Bear in mind that the panel will always inspect the property, so make sure it is in good condition.

- The panel will not take future works into account when assessing the rent (i.e. they will not assess a higher rent because you have planned substantial improvements).

- If improvements/repairs are being done at the property, the landlord can (and should) ask the Committee to adjourn the assessment until they are completed (because the assessed rent will probably be low if the inspection takes place while works are being carried out).

- The panel will disregard the effect of any improvements made by the tenant, any deterioration in the property caused by the tenant, and the effect of any service charges for which the landlord is responsible. Thus the tenant will not be penalised by having his rent increased because he has carried out improvements, neither can he take advantage of his own neglect of the property by being able to claim a lower rent.

- The panel cannot take the personal circumstances of either the landlord or the tenant into account – their job is to determine the market rent.

- Evidence of the rental of lettings of a similar type in the locality (for example, in the same street) will be very useful to the panel – they will need to know the type of tenancy, its terms, the size of the property let, the rent, and what is included in the letting (for example, if it is furnished or unfurnished, and if furnished, what is included).

- The panel will take particular note of very recent lettings, bearing in mind that the market can fluctuate over a short period.

- Advertisements for rented properties in the local paper will be of limited value, as the panel will have no evidence that these properties will actually achieve a tenant at the advertised rent.

- Bear in mind that a house will achieve a higher rental value overall if let on a room-by-room basis, with each tenant having his own tenancy agreement, as opposed to being let as one property under one tenancy agreement with all tenants having joint and several liability for the whole of the rent.

Once the panel has made its decision, it will provide both parties with a decision sheet. It will also give a statement of its reasons for coming to its decision.

There is a right of appeal from the panel's decision to the High Court, and from there to the Court of Appeal. However, you can only appeal the panel's decision on the basis that it has wrongly interpreted the law, not because you disagree with the way that they have interpreted the facts. This procedure is of course expensive and time-consuming and it unlikely to be followed by the small landlord.

If you are unhappy with the administration of panel cases you can complain to the Parliamentary Ombudsman. However, he will not look at the actual decision reached by the panel, just the procedures that were used to reach that decision.

Repairing duties/access

All landlords have the right to obtain access to the property to inspect its condition but, other than in cases of extreme emergency, this must not be without the tenant's knowledge and consent. Unauthorised access by the landlord may be deemed trespass and he may also fall foul of the harassment legislation.

It is important that the property is maintained in good repair throughout the tenancy (or at least those parts for which the landlord has responsibility).

If it is not, the tenant will be able to bring proceedings in the county court for a court order compelling the landlord to do the repairs, or he may be entitled to do the work himself and deduct the (reasonable) cost from the rent.

The tenant will be able to use the fact of the disrepair to defend any legal proceedings the landlord may bring, for example to obtain a possession order on the grounds of rent arrears.

The tenant, if financially eligible, will be often able to get Legal Aid. If he is successful in any legal proceedings, the landlord will also normally be ordered to pay the tenant's legal costs, which could be substantial.

A local authority has the right to enforce basic standards by serving a repairs notice on the landlord. If the landlord refuses to do the work, the local authority can ultimately do the works themselves and claim the cost from the landlord. Alternatively, they can obtain a demolition order.

It is important therefore that all complaints by tenants are dealt with promptly and that the property is regularly inspected and repairs carried out as necessary. However, a landlord cannot be required by a tenant to *improve* a property (unless it falls short of the basic standards): for example, a tenant cannot insist on normal windows being double-glazed. Also, the legislation provides that the character and prospective life-span of a property and the locality in which it is situated will affect the standard of repair required. The standard will therefore be different for quality housing in a 'good' neighbourhood, than for poor housing in a run-down district.

HMO properties

If you have an HMO you will in addition to the above, need to comply with the management standards (see page 17). This can involve quite a lot of work. For example:

- You will probably find that light bulbs will need constant replacement, as tenants often leave them on all

Tip

If a landlord has an obligation to repair or the right to enter and repair (which is usual), then he may be liable to a passer-by or an adjoining owner if damage is caused, **even if he does not know of the problem.**

the time. Some landlords find that it is more economical to have fluorescent lights fitted in the hallways, which are much cheaper to run if left on permanently.

- HMO tenants sometimes just dump their rubbish outside their own door rather than put it outside so the bin men can collect it. It is often simpler to put the rubbish outside yourself, and to bag it if this is necessary. If you do not, rubbish may accumulate and upset other tenants or neighbours.

- You may also have a problem with the bin men who may refuse to collect more than two bags per house, even though this house is now an HMO. It is best to tell the local authority refuse collection department that the property is now an HMO with a certain number of units, and they will tell the bin men, rather than tell the bin men yourself. You may have to tell the department a number of times before the message gets through!

You will need to inspect HMO properties more frequently than other properties, ideally at least once a week.

Housing Benefit

You will need to keep an eye on the property and inform the Benefit Office if the tenant vacates or if his circumstances change. Keep a record of when the tenant needs to re-apply for Benefit and make sure that he does so.

New tenancy agreements

When a fixed term comes to an end, you may wish to grant the tenant a new fixed term. It is a good idea to do this, as you can then use this as a method of increasing the rent (see 'Rent Matters' above). You can also incorporate new terms in the agreement. You may wish to do this as a result of new legislation, or to protect yourself against a problem you have encountered. If you have a number of rented properties, it is a good idea to have a standard tenancy agreement which you review from time to time to take account of these matters.

Law Pack tenancy agreements are periodically reviewed and updated to take account of legislation. Landlord associations will also periodically review their agreements. It is best therefore to buy new agreements rather than just photocopying an old agreement which may be out of date. For example, tenancy agreements have had to be reviewed recently to take account of the Unfair Contract Terms Regulations.

Tax considerations

Tax and financial matters are not considered in detail in this book and landlords are advised to seek professional advice from an accountant. Tax matters change annually and it is important that landlords are aware of the current regulations. However, the following comments may give some initial assistance.

Tip

A useful guide called 'Taxation of Rents' can be obtained free of charge from the Inland Revenue.

A landlord must inform the Inland Revenue that he is starting a rental business no later than 6th October after the end of the relevant tax year. As the Inland Revenue can make random enquiries and/or specific enquiries of tax payers at any time, it is essential that proper records are kept, as well as all invoices, receipts, and bank statements.

Income tax

Income from lettings is liable to income tax and is assessed under Schedule A. This includes income from all rented properties, any separate charges made to tenants for hiring furniture, service charges, and receipts from any insurance policy regarding non-payment of rent. It does not, however, include deposits which are refundable to the tenant at the end of the tenancy. Nor does it include charges for any additional services such as meals or laundry, which will normally be treated as a separate trading enterprise and taxable under Schedule D. Interest on rent paid late is also assessed under Schedule D.

You are able to offset against tax, expenses incurred wholly and exclusively for the purpose of the rental business. This does not include your time, but can include wages paid to staff. It can also include interest payments on loans for the purchase of properties and/or its contents, or for repair work and all general expenses involved in running the rental business such as advertising,

Council Tax, water rates, insurance premiums, repairs, finance costs, travelling expenses, most legal expenses, etc. Be sure to keep proper records of all your expenses, and all receipts and invoices. You may also be able to offset some capital expenses by way of a capital allowance.

The outlay for providing furniture and furnishings for furnished properties is regarded as a capital expense. However, a landlord is entitled to either deduct from income a wear-and-tear allowance of 10% of the rent, net of Council Tax, water bills, heat and light and any similar charges which would normally be borne by the tenant, or he can deduct the full costs of renewing (but not the initial cost of) individual items as and when the expenditure is incurred. But the landlord has to use the same method consistently and cannot change from year to year.

Capital gains tax

The gain on the sale of one's own home is normally exempt from this, but the gain on the sale of an investment property is taxable. If the taxpayer has been letting his own home during an absence, for example, while working abroad, the exemption is not normally jeopardised.

Expenditure on capital improvements are tax deductible. The taxable gain is also subject to an indexation allowance which strips out the inflationary element of the gain, and the indexed gain is tapered from the third year of ownership. There is then an annual exemption against capital gains, which at the time of writing is £7,200. Capital gains are currently taxed as if they were the top slice of a taxpayer's income for the year.

VAT

Lettings are currently exempt from VAT, unless they are holiday lettings. Holiday lettings will be treated in the same way as any other business which is subject to VAT. Your local VAT office will advise you.

Note

If you are letting a room in your own home there is a substantial tax allowance, currently £4,250, before tax is payable.

Note

Landlords should **not** rely on these notes alone when dealing with their tax affairs. They are intended as helpful comments only and not as a definitive guide. Tax matters change annually and it is essential that landlords obtain up-to-date professional advice to ensure that they are complying with the law.

7

Problem tenants

A landlord says ...

'If a tenant is always complaining, he is usually working up to non-payment of rent.'

Take action quickly

It is essential that all problems with tenants are dealt with quickly. If you ignore them they will just get worse. It is also wise to avoid a confrontation with tenants. If they have a complaint, try to put it right immediately. If the complaint is unreasonable, negotiate with them.

Landlord's duty to other tenants (covenant of quiet enjoyment)

If a landlord has other tenants nearby, he will owe them a duty of care under the covenant of quiet enjoyment (discussed in chapter 6). If some tenants are causing a disturbance he will therefore have a duty to do something about it. In extreme cases he may need to evict them. This is particularly important in HMOs.

Tip

If you believe a tenant is going to visit his local housing advice officer to complain, go down there yourself first and ask for advice about how to deal with your problems with the tenant. If you get your story in first and the housing officer sees that you are a reasonable person, he is less likely to write threatening letters to you.

Gas safety

Problems may occur when a tenant refuses access to a landlord to enable him to carry out the annual gas inspection. In the event of an incident, it will be for the landlord (or his managing agent) to show that he has taken all reasonable steps to meet his legal duties (and to avoid being prosecuted and fined). A suggested procedure is as follows:

► Tell the tenant when the inspection test will take place and give a telephone number to contact if this time is inconvenient, so another appointment can be arranged.

► If no communication is received from the tenant and the inspector is not able to gain access, write a letter to the tenant explaining that a gas safety check is a legal requirement and that it is for the tenant's own safety. Give the tenant an opportunity to make another appointment or suggest a further appointment.

► If after, say, 21 days, the tenant still fails to contact you or allow access, send a further letter, reiterating the importance of the test and asking that the tenant contact you urgently to arrange an appointment within a specified period (say 14 days).

► You should not use force to gain access to the property.

► If after three attempts you are still unable to gain access to have the safety check done, contact your local Health & Safety Executive.

► Threats of violence from the tenant will justify cutting short this process.

Records (giving the date and time and any other details) should be kept of all visits to the property and copies should be kept of all correspondence sent to the tenant.

Harassment legislation

It is beyond the scope of this book to consider harassment legislation in detail. Essentially, the legislation provides that harassment can be both a criminal offence and entitles the tenant to bring civil proceedings for an injunction and/or damages.

• **Criminal prosecutions** are normally brought by local authorities after tenants have been to them to complain. They will always write to the landlord first, however, so any correspondence received from them should be treated seriously.

Tip

If a landlord thinks that any gas appliances are faulty and/or there is a gas escape, he should contact Transco on 0800 111999 who have statutory rights of entry and powers of disconnection.

- **Civil proceedings** will be brought by the tenants themselves, usually with Legal Aid. They can prove extremely expensive for landlords, because if the tenant wins, the landlord will not only have to pay damages but also the tenant's legal costs.

The following are examples of actions which will entitle tenants and/or local authorities to invoke the legislation:

- Actual physical eviction of tenants from residential property by landlords. **Eviction of tenants should only ever be done by a court bailiff pursuant to a court order.**

- Threats of, or actual, violence and/or verbal abuse.

- Removal of doors, windows, and other items from the property.

- Disconnection of services, such as gas and electricity.

- Entering the property without the tenant's consent.

- Any act which is likely to cause the tenant to give up his occupancy of the property (even if this is not the landlord's intention).

Many landlords feel extremely frustrated by this legislation, when they see the tenants living in their property without paying rent, perhaps causing damage to the property, and using it for illegal purposes. However horrendous the tenant's conduct though, the landlord must always follow the correct procedures and should **never** resort to self-help measures. There are legal remedies available to deal with tenants who behave badly, although unfortunately they do take some time. If a landlord does not follow the proper procedure, he can find it an extremely expensive exercise.

An example:

A landlord lets a flat to a young lady. She only pays the first month's rent. She then starts behaving badly, she has loud parties and the neighbours complain. Her boyfriend causes a disturbance at the property on several occasions and kicks one of the doors in. The police are called in several times. The landlord goes round several times to ask for the rent. He tells her that unless she pays the rent and behaves properly she will have to go. On at least one occasion he loses his temper and shouts at her. One week he finds that she is not at the property. He continues to visit the property but she is never there. After about three weeks he suspects that she has left and uses his keys to gain entry. The house is in a dirty condition and it is obvious that no-one has been there for some time. It is full of rubbish and there is mouldy food in the kitchen. He finds some of her personal things, such as a purse with £5 in it, clothes in the wardrobe and in the chest of drawers in the bedroom, and some videos in the lounge. However, he decides that she has left, bags up all the items left in the property, and changes the locks. None of the items left being saleable, he dumps them (apart from the money in the purse which he takes against the rent arrears), re-decorates the flat, and then re-lets it to another tenant.

Two months later he learns of a scene at the flat when the young lady tries to gain entry and is refused by the new tenant. He is subsequently served with a county court summons for damages for harassment and unlawful eviction together with a claim for compensation for her property, and a notice stating that she has been awarded Legal Aid. He loses the case and is ordered to pay compensation to the tenant, although the sum is reduced to take account of her unpaid rent and damage to the flat. He also has to pay her legal costs which run into several thousand pounds, as well as his own solicitor's bill.

This landlord would also have been vulnerable to a prosecution for unlawful eviction.

Had the landlord followed the correct procedure and obtained a possession order, the tenant would not have been able to make any claim against him. He would have been out of pocket but the sums involved would have been far less.

Every landlord who lets property for any period of time is bound to have at least one bad tenant. All you can do is be careful in your choice of tenant, act swiftly to resolve any problems, and if the problem cannot be resolved, follow the correct legal procedures for evicting the tenant. Unfortunately, having the occasional bad tenant is just part of the job of being a landlord and when it happens to you, you just have to accept this and deal with it in a professional way.

A landlord says ...

'A tenant who is trouble at the beginning of a tenancy will continue to be trouble to the end.'

Evicting tenants

When evicting tenants, you need to have a 'ground' for eviction and to have served the proper notice on the tenant before legal proceedings are started.

Grounds for possession

These are divided into mandatory grounds and discretionary grounds. It is strongly recommended that landlords only ever evict if they have mandatory grounds for possession, as this means that the judge has no alternative but to grant an order for possession. If only discretionary grounds are claimed, the tenant may be able to get Legal Aid to defend the proceedings and you will be faced with a large legal bill if you lose.

There are several mandatory grounds for possession but the ones that are most commonly used are:

- **The shorthold ground.** If a tenancy is an assured shorthold tenancy, the landlord is entitled to a possession order as of right, after the fixed term has expired, provided the proper form of notice (called a section 21 notice) is served.

- **The owner occupier ground.** (Ground 1) Provided a notice has been served on the tenant before the tenancy is entered into, stating that possession may be granted on this ground, the landlord is entitled to possession as of right provided the proper form of notice (called a section 8 notice) has been served.

- **Serious rent arrears.** (Ground 8) Provided that both at the time of service of the notice (a section 8 notice) and at the time of the court hearing, the tenant is in arrears of rent of more than eight weeks or two months, the landlord will be entitled to possession as of right.

There are some other mandatory grounds but these are unusual and are not discussed in this book.

Most tenancies are shorthold nowadays, and if a tenant proves unsatisfactory it is best to simply serve the section 21 notice and then issue proceedings under the shorthold ground at the end of the term. If the tenant's behaviour is so serious that you cannot wait, inform the police (if appropriate) and take legal advice immediately.

Notices

Service of the correct notice (in writing) is a pre-requisite for obtaining a possession order. If you cannot prove that this was done, you will not (except in exceptional circumstances) obtain your possession order.

The correct notice to be served will depend upon the ground you are using and whether the fixed term has expired or not.

- **Shorthold ground where the fixed term has not yet ended.** Here the notice must be for a period of at least two months and must end at or after the end of the fixed term. So for example, for a fixed term of six months starting on 1st January, if the notice is served on 2nd January, the notice period must end on or after 30th June (which means that you cannot issue proceedings until after that date). If it is served on 1st May it must end on or after 31st July. This form of notice can be served up to and including 30th June (when it would end on or after 31st August).

- **Shorthold ground after the fixed term has ended.** Here the period of the notice must be at least two months and it must end on the last day of a 'period of the tenancy'. To continue with the example above, the periodic tenancy will start on 1st July and, presuming that rent is payable monthly, the period will be from month to month and will end on the last day in the month. So if the notice is served on 5th July, it must end on 30th September.

- **All other grounds.** Here the notice must be issued in the form prescribed by section 8 of the Act. If you are serving the notice under Ground 1, it will need to be a two-month notice, if you are serving notice under Ground 8 it is a two-week notice.

If you are not sure what you are doing, you should get a solicitor to draft the notice for you. It is essential that the notice is correct as otherwise you will not be granted a possession order at court.

Always keep a record of the date and time of service of the notice, the method of service (by post, personally, through the letter box), and the name of the person who served it. It is recommended that notices are served by putting them (in an envelope addressed to the tenant) through the letter box of the property yourself, rather than sending them by post, as this way the tenant cannot say that they got lost in the post. Recorded delivery is not advised as the tenant can refuse to accept delivery.

Possession proceedings

For ATs and ASTs, there are two types of possession proceedings you can use, the 'normal' proceedings and the (so called) 'accelerated' proceedings.

- **Accelerated proceedings.** These can only be used if your ground for possession is either the shorthold ground or the owner occupier ground (Ground 1). It cannot be used to claim rent arrears. It is quicker because the evidence is given by way of a written statement to the court and there is no court hearing. If successful, you will get an order for possession (normally enforceable 14 days after the order was made) and an order that the tenant pay 'fixed costs' (if you are acting in person this will just be the court fee). From the issue of proceedings to receipt of the order for possession, these proceedings normally take between six to 10 weeks.

- **Normal proceedings.** These involve a court hearing where you will have to attend and present your case to the judge. However, you will also normally be entitled to a money judgment for any rent arrears due at the date of the hearing, and an order that the tenant pays future rent until he vacates the property. If the rent arrears remain unpaid you can enforce this judgement through the courts. You will also be entitled to an order for costs (if you are acting in person this will normally be limited to the court fee and your costs of attending the hearing).

Unless you are very certain of what you are doing, it is really best to instruct a solicitor should it become necessary to evict

Tip

Make sure the property is in good repair before issuing proceedings for serious rent arrears. If it is not, the tenant will be able to bring a counterclaim against you (often with the benefit of Legal Aid) which may prevent you from getting possession and also make you liable for an award of damages and an order to pay his legal costs.

your tenant. Judges do not like making possession orders and will usually refuse to do so, unless a landlord has got his paperwork right. If you make a mistake, a tenant will be able to defend (often with Legal Aid) and you may end up with no possession order and an order to pay the tenant's legal costs.

If you do instruct a solicitor, make sure he is one who is experienced in this type of work (many are not), and that you get a firm quotation for their costs before they do any work. The solicitor will need:

- The tenancy agreement.

- Copies of all notices served on the tenant.

- Details of how, when, and by whom the notices were served.

- Any correspondence with the tenant, and any other notes and paperwork.

- A schedule of the rent arrears (if you are claiming unpaid rent).

- A payment on account of costs.

Evicting Rent Act tenants

It is beyond the scope of this Guide to deal with the eviction of Rent Act tenants. If you wish to evict a Rent Act tenant, you should seek specialist legal advice.

Squatters and licensees

If the person occupying the property does not have a tenancy, then you will be able to use another form of possession proceedings. These proceedings are much quicker than those used for tenancies and you can sometimes obtain a possession order in less than two weeks. However it is not advisable for a landlord to bring this type of proceeding on his own unless he really knows what he is doing. It would be much better to instruct a reliable firm of solicitors, experienced in eviction work.

Enforcement of possession orders

Even if you have a possession order, you cannot enforce this other than through the court bailiff. Do **not** physically evict the tenant (or occupiers) yourself!

The possession order will give a date for possession. Unless specifically authorised by the court, you will have to wait until after this date before instructing the bailiffs. If the tenant is still in the property at that time, you will have to complete a request form and send this, together with the court fee, to court. It will normally take some weeks for an appointment to be arranged (unless you are evicting squatters, when the bailiffs usually act quickly). The bailiff always visits the property before fixing the appointment, to discuss the eviction with the occupiers.

When an appointment is made, you must always arrange for someone to attend with the bailiff and formally take possession from him. You should also arrange for a locksmith to be present to change the locks.

Excluded tenancies or licences

If the letting is one of the following:

(i)   to a lodger in your own home;

(ii)   to a tenant of a flat in the same building as the land-lord's main or only home (unless a purpose built block of flats);

(iii) a holiday let;

there is no duty on you to obtain an order for possession for the purposes of the criminal law.

You must, however, tell the occupier in writing that you want him to leave and give the occupier a reasonable period of time to vacate. For (ii) above, you should serve a formal Notice to Quit in the proper form (the notice period must be for a minimum of four weeks ending on the last day of a period of the tenancy or at the end of any fixed term).

However, if it is clear that the tenant is not going to vacate voluntarily and will resist any attempts of eviction, you should consult a solicitor. You may still have to issue possession proceedings, for example of the type discussed above for squatters and licensees.

Money claims

There may be times when landlords wish to claim for rent, but do not want or need to claim for possession. For example, if the tenant has already left the property, or if the tenant (or Housing Benefit) is paying rent but there are a few weeks rent outstanding, perhaps relating to the period before housing benefit started. Also, the landlord will have a claim against the tenant if he has vacated the property leaving it in a poor condition, and the damage deposit is insufficient to cover the landlord's costs of putting things right.

Many landlords are also defendants in proceedings brought by tenants for the return of their damage deposit where there is a dispute about the landlord's entitlement to retain this.

Money claims should be brought in the county court and, if (as is usual) they are for sums of less than £5,000, they will be dealt with by the small claims procedure.

When bringing proceedings against tenants, landlords should ensure that they have evidence to support each and every element of their claim. For claiming rent arrears they will need a detailed rent statement showing how the rent arrears accrued. Claims for interest should be kept entirely separate and should not be included in this schedule. For claims for damages, landlords will need either an estimate or an invoice for the cost of all items/work claimed. If witnesses are to be used, you will need to have a written statement of what they are going to say, which should be signed and dated. They will, however, usually still need to attend the hearing. You will also need to prepare a written statement of your own evidence.

The county court now has a special standard form of 'directions' for defended claims relating to damage deposits and damage claims, which reads as follows:

> 1   Each party shall deliver to every other party and to the court office copies of all documents on which he intends to rely at the hearing. These may include:

Note

Landlords who are participating in the Tenancy Deposit Scheme will be able to refer any dispute to the Housing Ombudsman for adjudication.

- the tenancy agreement and any inventory,

- the rent book or other evidence of rent and other payments made by the claimant/defendant to the claimant/defendant,

- photographs,

- witness statements,

- invoices or estimates for work and goods.

2   The copies shall be delivered no later than (either a specific date or 14 days before the hearing).

3   The original documents shall be brought to the hearing.

4   The claimant/defendant shall deliver with his copy documents a list showing each item of loss or damage for which he claims the claimant/defendant ought to pay, and the amount he claims for the replacement or repair.

5   The parties shall before the hearing date try to agree about the nature and cost of any repairs and replacements needed, subject to the court's decision about any other issue in the case.

6   Signed statements setting out the evidence of all witnesses on whom each party intends to rely shall be prepared and included in the documents mentioned in paragraph 1. This includes the evidence of the parties themselves and of any other witness whether or not he is going to come to court to give evidence.

7   The parties should note that:

a) in deciding the case the judge may find it helpful to have photographs showing the condition of the property,

b) the judge may decide not to take into account a document or the evidence of a witness if no copy of that document or no copy of a statement or report by that witness has been supplied to the other parties.

For more information about practice and procedure in the Small Claims Court, readers are referred to the **Law Pack** *Small Claims Guide*.

8

At the end of
a tenancy

When does the tenancy end? ———————

In practice, in one of the following two situations:

1.   At the end of the term when the tenant leaves voluntarily, or

2.   When an order for possession has been made by the court.

Tip

If a tenant hands you his keys before the term has ended saying he wants to give up his tenancy, make it very clear that you do not accept his surrender, and that you will hold him responsible for the rent until another tenant is found. If you do not do this you may be deemed to have accepted the surrender.

Normally the tenant leaves voluntarily – to use legal terminology, he 'surrenders' the tenancy. However, a tenant cannot force you to accept a surrender before the end of the term. If he leaves mid-way through the term, you can still claim rent from him and if he does not pay, obtain a county court judgment (provided you have his new address or a contact address). You will not be able to claim rent from him after you have re-let the property to another tenant (apart from existing arrears).

Problems can arise when it is not certain whether a tenant has left or not. Obviously a landlord will want to re-let a property as soon as possible, particularly if there are rent arrears. But a landlord must be extremely careful in these circumstances when re-entering the property, as he may be vulnerable to a charge of unlawful eviction.

You will usually be safe to re-possess if:

•   The fixed term has come to an end, and

- **All** the tenant's possessions have gone, particularly if the keys are left in the property.

Be very careful if the tenant has left items at the property, particularly if the term has not come to an end. The tenant may be on a long holiday, or be in hospital, or prison. If it is not absolutely clear that the tenant has vacated permanently, you should keep out of the property and obtain a possession order through the courts. See chapter 7.

Obviously you should only be considering re-entering and repossessing if the rent is in arrears. If the rent is paid up, you should not, except in the case of emergency, enter the property at all without the tenant's permission.

Hand-over procedure

When it is time for the tenant to go, you should arrange for an appointment with him at the property. You should then check over the contents of the property with him, using the inventory, and also the condition of the property. Usually you should be able to decide there and then whether you will need to make any retention from the damage deposit and if so how much this should be for. The damage deposit should then be returned to the tenant as soon as possible, however, not until after:

- the tenants have vacated the property **and** returned the keys; and

- you are sure that there is not going to be any claw-back from the Housing Benefit office.

Remember when making retentions from the damage deposit, that you must allow for fair wear and tear. The property will normally have been occupied for a long period and it is unrealistic to expect it to be in the same pristine condition that it was, at the start of the tenancy. If it is left in a dirty condition, you are entitled to claim for the reasonable costs of having the property cleaned. Keep all estimates and invoices, so you can justify all sums deducted from the damage deposit in the event of a claim against you for example in the county court.

Tip

Do not return the damage deposit until after you have done a careful inspection of the property – once you have returned the damage deposit it is very difficult, if not impossible, to get it back.

A letting agent says...

'We find that most problems with damage deposits are caused by landlords being unreasonable about damage due to wear and tear.'

Tip

Try to obtain a forwarding address for the tenants. You may need it later if you have a claim against them.

Death of a tenant

What happens if an AT or an AST tenant dies? If he is one of joint tenants, the tenancy will simply continue in the name of the other joint tenant/s. If the tenant is a sole tenant, then as discussed in chapter 1, the tenancy will normally pass to the tenant's spouse, or to a member of his family, under his will, or under the intestacy rules. If the tenancy passes to anyone other than the tenant's spouse, then the landlord has a mandatory ground for possession, provided proceedings are issued within 12 months of the tenant's death.

If the tenancy is a Rent Act tenancy, then the tenancy will pass as above to the spouse, family member, etc. The succession rights of tenants are stronger under Rent Act tenancies and there is no mandatory ground for possession.

It is beyond the scope of this book to consider the succession rights of tenants in detail. Landlords are advised to seek further advice from a solicitor, particularly if the tenant is a Rent Act tenant.

After the tenant has gone

Utilities – Make sure that a meter reading is done before the property is re-let.

Post – If you do not have a forwarding address for the old tenant, do not keep or throw post away; return everything, marked 'gone away'.

You will then have to clean the property, re-decorate if necessary, and start all over again!

Appendix 1

Useful addresses and telephone numbers

Association of Residential Letting Agents (ARLA)
ARLA Administration
Maple House
53–55 Woodside Road
Amersham   Tel: 01923 896555
Bucks HP6 6AA   www.arla.co.uk/

Transco
0800 111999

Companies House
Crown Way
Cardiff   Tel: 029 2038 0801
CF14 3UZ   www.companieshouse.gov.uk

Corgi
1 Elmwood
Chineham Business Park   Tel: 01256 372200
Crockford Lane, Basingstoke   Fax: 01256 708144
Hampshire RG24 8WG   www.corgi-gas.co.uk/

Health and Safety Executive Books
PO Box 1999
Sudbury   Tel: 01787 881 165
Suffolk CO10 6FS   www.hse.gov.uk/

Health and Safety Executive Gas Safety Advice Line
0800 300363

Incorporated Society of Valuers & Surveyors (ISVA)
3 Cadogan Gate   Tel 020 7235 2282
London   Fax 020 7235 4390
SW1X 0AS   www.isva.co.uk

Independent Housing Ombudsman Limited
Norman House
105–109 Strand   Tel: 020 7379 1754
London WC2R 0AA   Fax: 020 7836 3900

Inland Revenue Stamp Duty Helpline
Tel: 0845 603 0135   www.inlandrevenue.gov.uk

National Federation of Residential Landlords
Sackville Place   Tel: 01603 762980
44-48 Magdalen Chambers   Fax: 01603 762981
Norwich NR3 1JU   www.nfrl.org.uk

National Inspection Council for Electrical Installation Contracting (NICEIC)
Vintage House   Tel: 020 7564 2323
37 Albert Embankment   Fax: 020 7564 2370
London SE1 7UJ   www.niceic.org.uk/

Parliamentary Ombudsman
Office of the Parliamentary Commissioner for Administration
Millbank Tower
Millbank   Tel:0845 0154033
London SW1P 4QP   Fax: 020 7217 4160

Office of Fair Trading
Fleetbank House
2–6 Salisbury Square   Tel: 020 7211 8000
London EC4Y 8JX   www.oft.gov.uk/index.htm

Rent Service
1st Floor, Clifton House
87–113 Euston Road   Tel: 020 7388 4838
London NW1 2RA   Fax: 020 7388 0285

Royal Institution of Chartered Surveyors (RICS)
Parliament Square   Tel: 020 7222 7000
12 Great George Street   Fax: 020 7222 9430
London SW1P 3AD   www.rics.org.uk

Unfair Contract Terms Unit
Office of Fair Trading
Room 505, Field House
15–25 Bream's Buildings   Tel: 020 7211 8446
London EC4A 1PR   Fax: 020 7211 8404

Appendix 2

CORGI
The Council for Registered Gas Installers

By law, anyone carrying out gas-related work must be Corgi-registered. To comply with the Gas Safety Regulations, landlords must ensure that the person who does the safety checks and any work is Corgi-registered, and is also registered to do the type of work required.

Corgi-registered installers have to undergo rigorous training and regular re-training and inspection before they obtain their competency certificates. Every registered Corgi installer must have a Corgi ID card. You should ask to see this before any work is done. Their registration is limited to the types of work they are qualified to do, details of which are set out on the reverse of their ID card.

If you are unhappy about the standard of work done by a Corgi-registered installer, Corgi will often agree to inspect this free of charge, as part of their monitoring programme. They can be contacted on 01256 372499.

Index

In this Index, landlords and letting, the principal subjects of the text, are classified under other terms. Statutes are in *italic* type, locators in **bold** type indicate a more detailed section and the letter 'e' after a locator indicates an example.

tenancies
  ATs *see* ATs (assured
    tenancies)
    ASTs *see* ASTs (assured
      shorthold tenancies)
  existing on purchased
    properties 15–16
  former, final checks 93
  legal interest 1–2
  location factors 11
  Rent Act *see* Rent Act
    tenancies
  succession 8, 93
  surrender 2–3, **91–2**
terms
  clarity 49

commencement date 50–1
fairness 49
fixed **6**, 51–2
  eviction notices 84
  renewal 75–6
periodic 6
written vs oral 47–8
Trading Standards Office,
  powers 30

Unfair Terms Regulations 48–9
universities, advertising to find
  tenants 35–6
use of property restrictions 58

water bills **28**, 53

Notes

Ten aggrement,
list of rules.

Notes

Notes

Notes

Law Pack tenancy and other Form Packs...

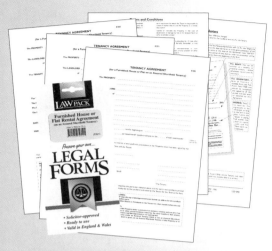

England and Wales Form Packs

Furnished House or Flat Rental Agreement
(on an Assured Shorthold Tenancy)
Code F201 • £3.99 • ISBN 1 902646 09 6

Unfurnished House or Flat Rental Agreement
(on an Assured Shorthold Tenancy)
Code F202 • £3.99 • ISBN 1 902646 10 X

House or Flat Share Agreement
(for a room in a furnished house or flat with a resident owner)
Code F203 • £3.99 • ISBN 1 902646 08 8

House or Flat Share Agreement
(for a room in a furnished house or flat with a non-resident owner)
Code F204 • £3.99 • ISBN 1 902646 07 X

Holiday Letting Agreement
(for holiday lets of furnished property)
Code F213 • £3.99 • ISBN 1 898217 53 X

Notice to Terminate
(for use with either Rental or House/Flat Share Agreements)
Code F206 • £3.99 • ISBN 1 902646 12 6

Rent Book
(records rent paid – required by law if rent is paid weekly)
Code F207 • £3.99 • ISBN 1 898217 27 0

Household Inventory
Code F208 • £3.99 • ISBN 1 898217 32 7

Last Will & Testament (for gifts not in trust)
Code F216 • £3.99 • ISBN 1 902646 14 2

General Power of Attorney (to authorise another to act on your behalf with full legal authority)
Code F220 • £3.99 • ISBN 1 902646 16 9

Living Will
(your advance instructions on medical treatment)
Code F212 • £3.99 • ISBN 1 898217 52 1

Cohabitation Agreement (for unmarried partners)
Code F217 • £3.99 • ISBN 1 898217 73 4

Employment Contract
(standard agreement between employer and employee)
Code F209 • £3.99 • ISBN 1 902646 11 8

Builder/Decorator Contract
(details work to be done, time-scale, payment etc.)
Code F210 • £3.99 • ISBN 1 898217 42 4

Business Partnership Agreement
(contract between individuals starting partnership)
Code F211 • £3.99 • ISBN 1 902646 15 0

Sales Representative Agreement
(sets out products, territory, commission etc.)
Code F218 • £3.99 • ISBN 1 898217 78 5

Anti-Gazumping Agreement
(for exclusivity before exchange when buying property)
Code F214 • £3.99 • ISBN 1 898217 58 0

Pools Syndicate Agreement
(safeguards any winnings of group football pools players)
Code F219 • £3.99 • ISBN 1 898217 83 1

Vehicle Purchase Agreement
(for private sale of car, van or motorcycle)
Code F221 • £3.99 • ISBN 1 902646 31 2

National Lottery Syndicate Agreement
(safeguards any winnings of group Lottery players)
Code J215 • £3.99 • ISBN 1 898217 93 9

... to order, simply call 020 7940 7000 or visit www.lawpack.co.uk

More books from Law Pack...

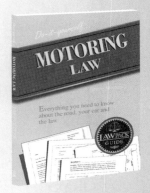

Probate

What happens when someone dies, with or without leaving a Will, and their estate needs to be dealt with? Probate is the process whereby the deceased's executors apply for authority to handle the deceased's assets. This Guide provides the information and instructions needed to obtain a grant of probate, or grant of letters of administration, and administer an estate without the expense of a solicitor.

Code B409 • ISBN 1 902646 27 4 • 246 x 189mm
96 pp • £9.99 • 2nd Edition

Divorce

File your own undefended divorce and save legal fees! This Guide explains the process from filing your petition to final decree. Even if there are complications such as young children or contested grounds this Guide will save you time and money.

Code B404 • ISBN 1 902646 05 3 • A4 PB
120 pp • £9.99 • 2nd Edition

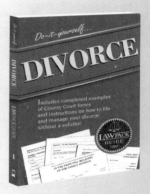

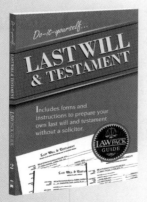

Last Will & Testament

With the help of this Guide writing a Will can be a straightforward matter. It takes the reader step by step through the process of drawing up a Will, while providing background information and advice. Will forms, completed examples and checklists included.

Code B403 • ISBN 1 902646 06 1 • A4 PB
80 pp • £9.99 • 2nd Edition

... to order, simply call 020 7940 7000 or visit www.lawpack.co.uk

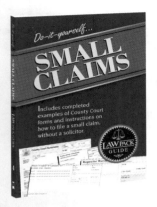

Small Claims

If you want to take action to recover a debt, resolve a contract dispute or make a personal injury claim, you can file your own small claim without a solicitor. This Guide includes clear instructions and advice on how to handle your own case and enforce judgment.

Code B406 • ISBN 1 902646 04 5 • A4 PB
96 pp • £9.99 • 2nd Edition

Personnel Manager

A Form Book of more than 200 do-it-yourself forms, contracts and letters to help you manage your personnel needs more effectively. As employment laws and codes of practice increasingly affect the workplace, good, efficient record-keeping is essential for any employer, large or small. There's no quicker or easier way to 'get it in writing' than using *Personnel Manager*. Areas covered: Recruitment & Hiring, Employment Contracts & Agreements, Handling New Employees, Personnel Management, Performance Evaluation and Termination of Employment.

Code B417 • ISBN 1 902646 02 9 • A4 PB
246 pp • £17.99 • 2nd Edition

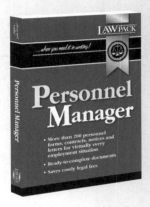

Company Secretary

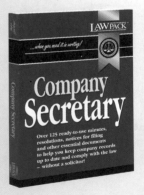

What every busy company secretary or record-keeper needs. Maintaining good, up-to-date records of company meetings and resolutions is not only good practice but also a legal requirement, however small your company is. This Form Book makes compiling minutes of board and shareholder meetings straightforward. It includes more than 125 commonly-required resolutions and minutes: all that a limited company is likely to need.

Code B416 • ISBN 1 902646 19 3 • A4 PB
190 pp • £17.99 • 2nd Edition

... to order, simply call 020 7940 7000 or visit www.lawpack.co.uk